Nobel Costa Rica

N🕮BEL
COSTA RICA

*A Timely Report on our Peaceful
Pro-Yankee, Central American Neighbor*

Seth Rolbein

A
JOAN
Kahn
BOOK

ST. MARTIN'S PRESS
NEW YORK

Design by Jennifer Dossin

Library of Congress Cataloging-in-Publication Data

Rolbein, Seth.
    Nobel Costa Rica / Seth Rolbein.
      p. cm.
    "A Joan Kahn book."
    ISBN 0-312-02262-X
    1. Costa Rica—Politics and government—1986- 2. Arias Sánchez,
Oscar. I. Title.
F1548.2.R6 1988
972.86—dc19
                                                            88-11599
                                                                CIP

First Edition

10 9 8 7 6 5 4 3 2 1

This book is dedicated to fragile peace
and imperfect democracy.

ACKNOWLEDGMENTS

An extraordinary number of people helped make this book possible. Colleagues became friends, and friends became colleagues. Beyond the people quoted and discussed in the pages, most of whom were most gracious with their time and thoughts, I'd like to thank Linda Holland, Tom Cronin, Jeanne O'Neil, David Wood, Hugh Delios, Rick Holland, Seth Kantor, Ron Hutcheson, Mark Nelson, Foster and Nancy Phillips, Steve Schwadron, Amy Hilferty, Susan Steinway, Marvin and Eddie at La Cariari, and Joan Kahn for her vision and faith.

Nobel Costa Rica

CHAPTER ONE

Of Myths and Men

December 1, 1987. Downtown San José, Costa Rica's capital.

It was morning and so the sun had to be shining in the saturated azure of the sky above the Central Plateau, overexposing the shapes and colors of the city, carving dark shadows behind every corner, blazing through the stained glass of the Metropolitan Cathedral and illuminating the sacred interior. Shafts of light, suddenly colored and muted, poured past the rising smoke of incense and candles, angling from the vaulted ceiling, haloing the face of one worshiper in gold, capturing the hands of another in violet, caressing the crucifix of a third in ruby.

But television camera lights do not allow for such sub-

1

tlety, because video doesn't see much of anything in that kind of ethereal murkiness, in the dark moments where the suggestion of divinity works as the architect intended. And so the cathedral's dais, where New York's Cardinal John J. O'Connor stood, was bathed in white klieg lights, more like the street than the church, to ensure his speech was properly recorded.

As Cardinal O'Connor spoke, he seemed to be addressing different people at different moments. Sometimes it was the congregation spread out below (although his English was not understood by many). Sometimes it was the reporters hunched nearby, myself included. Sometimes it was Oscar Arias Sánchez, Costa Rica's celebrated young president, seated to one side, dressed in a conservative, impeccable suit, his black hair carefully combed, a short man by U.S. standards with a slight hunch to the shoulders that suggests a mock humility.

But most of all O'Connor was talking through the reporters to an international audience that might have included the Nobel Prize Committee in Oslo, Norway, or members of the United States Congress—whose Speaker of the House, Jim Wright, happened to be standing in the smaller side room of the cathedral. That mixture (or even uncertainty) of focus, of whom to talk to, is nothing new for Central America, where statements and actions have been framed, interpreted, and even controlled by North Americans and Europeans for many years.

"We cannot honor the anniversary of the abolition of the army without at the same time honoring this new movement for peace," Cardinal O'Connor said. "You have struck one match, you have lit one candle. You will develop a momentum for peace which will radiate through the region."

OF MYTHS AND MEN

"The abolition of the army," murmured one of the Texas press corps traveling with Speaker Wright, "that took place on December 1, 1948, am I right? Then this is the thirty-ninth anniversary, not the fortieth as the press release says. Right?"

Right, but there was no time to explain why Costa Ricans might not worry too much whether it was the thirty-ninth or fortieth anniversary, because the service was breaking up and the real celebration was about to begin. President Arias, just days away from his trip to Europe to receive the Nobel Peace Prize, strode off the stage and to a small, old man who was sitting in an aisle seat. He looked familiar, like someone's grandfather, with a strong hooked nose over thin lips, high forehead with the remains of gray hair smoothed straight back, suit and tie and white shirt as befits a public ceremony. Someone's grandfather, yes, but, more properly, Costa Rica's grandfather—and Oscar Arias's political godfather.

Tears were streaming down the old man's face, and a white handkerchief in his shaking hand strayed to gray-blue eyes. That hand had held a sledgehammer thirty-nine years earlier and had used it to bash the top of the wall of the Costa Rican national barracks to symbolize the end of the military. Those gray-blue eyes had had the vision to do what no one else has ever done: win a revolution, abolish an army, voluntarily relinquish power to the rightfully elected president, and abide by free and fair elections every four years since. In historic terms, as far as one man can alter the direction of his nation and create a current that carries someone like Oscar Arias to the presidency, this small old man deserves to share space with the great names of the century.

And so Oscar Arias went first to José Figueres Ferrer

3

and helped him to his feet, all five feet three inches of him, all eighty-one years of him, and arm in arm they walked down the aisle of the cathedral and out to the crowds gathered on the steps. It was a sweet moment, a moment of which national myths are made, the founding father of the Second Republic with tears streaming down his face and a white hanky fluttering in his hand alongside the young president whose vision has catapulted Costa Rica into the international spotlight. It was akin to seeing time crumble, allowing George Washington, the revolutionary who knew how to lay down his weapons, to walk arm in arm with John Kennedy, the intellectual statesman of the New Frontier. It was the real reason why the actual year of Costa Rica's anniversary didn't matter. Whether thirty-nine years or forty years had passed, a historic circle had been closed, while time remained before the jet left for Oslo and before Don Pepe Figueres (the "Don" a title of respect, the "Pepe" an affectionate diminutive of *José*), could no longer participate in the ceremony.

"Viva Don Pepe!" yelled voices in the crowd.

"Viva Costa Rica!" shouted others.

Arias and Figueres walked slowly into the throng, joined by Speaker Wright and nearly a dozen United States congressmen who had been invited to celebrate the anniversary of the army's abolition. It was the briefest of whirlwind tours for the Speaker and his entourage, less than twenty-four hours, undertaken even though Mikhail Gorbachev was expected to arrive in Washington that week. But Jim Wright's being there showed the new symbolic level to which Arias has raised Costa Rica in the international consciousness. Just to make sure everyone got the message, though, the parade route was adorned with the symbols of Costa Rica's pacifism. Lining the path were children carrying long-stemmed flowers and banners that read *Costa Rica Ama La Paz* (Costa Rica loves peace). There was not a single uniformed officer or crowd-control policeman around, the closest thing being a group of Boy Scouts in their blue uniforms and yellow ties. Another band of teenagers wore T-shirts stenciled *Constructores de la Paz* (Peacemakers) and their job was to keep Avenida Dos clear enough for people to move toward the national museum. High school bands had assembled and the *oom-pa-pa* of their music began to urge the parade onward. Arias sends his children to the Lincoln School, and a picture of Abraham Lincoln bobbed over the marchers. Rows of Costa Rican flags were unfurled, and in the spirit of both the Boy Scouts and Abe Lincoln the flags were red, white, and blue.

The crush of the crowd and the mile-long walk were too much for Figueres, and so he was eased into the front seat of a car and slowly driven along the parade route. Tears still streaked his face as women brought him their babies to kiss and young men reached for his hand. I walked briefly alongside the car and talked with him about the book I would soon begin to write. I said I wanted the book to become a national biography, if such a thing were possible, that would try to explain why Costa Rica is a peaceful oasis in an isthmus of turmoil. While most international journalists have been flocking to Nicaragua or Panama to report on the violence and confrontation there, between the two countries is a nation that, in the bigger scheme of things, seems to hold the real promise of the region. Its culture by turns is familiar and foreign to North Americans but has almost always been misunderstood. And so I thought that a book about Costa Rica could turn on a few lights and make people understand that not all Central

America is some monolithic place of bananas, corruption, teetering revolutions, and prolonged war.

Don Pepe focused his gray-blue eyes on me, appraising me for a moment. "That's good to hear," he said, in his impeccable English. "We need that. Good luck." And then he leaned back, his eyes becoming hazy, as if even that short discussion was exhausting.

Behind his car walked the dignitaries. A *la tica* (the slang phrase meaning in Costa Rican fashion), the parade seemed to be moving more sideways than forward, but President Arias pretty much stuck to the middle of the road, not hamming it up as some politicians would. He is a shy man, perhaps the most self-contained political leader I have ever seen. I don't get the sense he needs to press the flesh or that his juices flow with the rush of the crowd; more, he seems to be on an individual quest, perhaps looking for his place in history. Few expected him to win the presidency in 1986. Many berated his thoughtful, somber, almost soporific campaign style. No one expected his combination of stubborn independence and a true statesman's vision. Even in the streets of San José, Oscar Arias continues to surprise people in the best of senses, managing, somehow, to exceed expectations. As the parade wiggled its way toward the national museum, the hot sun of midday beating down, Don Oscar offered another little surprise: He stopped at the curb for an *helado*, an ice cream cone, and rejoined the throng.

Arias, like the country he leads, works an extraordinary high-wire act: He is a reputable democratic leader walking amid the ashes of exploded oligarchies and war. He balances an armyless republic between Nicaragua and Panama, between Ortega and Noriega, between Nicaragua's *contras* and El Salvador's rebels. He desperately clings to a peculiarly Costa Rican concept of neutrality while deeply in debt, dependent on United States aid yet using the web of moral authority as a national safety net. The act is thrilling audiences the world over, not to mention offering the best opportunity in decades for a form of peaceful stability in Central America that includes at least a dash of social justice. It tends to play better on the road than at home: In politics, as in other things, familiarity breeds some contempt.

I first met President Arias near the end of his first year in office, in January 1987. It was his combination of intellect and grace that impressed me most, so much so that when I returned to the United States I did a dangerous thing for a journalist—unreservedly praised a politician, and a Central American one to boot. Within a year of that meeting, the Nobel Prize committee announced the selection of Oscar Arias Sánchez as the peace laureate of 1987. And so I watched this Costa Rican president suddenly catch the world's eye much as he had caught mine and continued trying to fit him into a complex puzzle of psychology, politics, and history, of Costa Rica, Central America, and the Western Hemisphere.

Watching Speaker Wright work the crowd was another kettle of fish. While Arias seemed to maintain an aura of privacy in the midst of everything, a personal bubble that had nothing to do with Secret Service agents or external events, Wright seemed to be straining to avoid any semblance of separation between himself and the crowd. It was a chance for him to practice the Spanish he had picked up in one of those intensive language courses the State Department runs for public officials, and he spoke in a Texan's flat accent, asking a young girl where she went to school and what was her favorite class. Even the protruding tufts of his eyebrows seemed to be straining forward, little political antennae in search of signals.

Wright owes Costa Rica something. The country's legitimacy allowed the Arias Peace Plan to emerge, and Wright's understanding of this raised him from a Texas pol with enough staying power to become Speaker of the House to an international statesman whose good instincts put the Reagan State Department to shame. What's more, Costa Rica's the kind of place where you can bring a dozen congressmen, walk in a parade, see Boy Scouts and pictures of Abraham Lincoln, talk to reasonable and rightfully elected officials (most of whom speak good English), admire a standard of living that makes San José look a lot more like San Antonio than Managua, and come back home after twenty hours filled with patriotic pride at the good that U.S. foreign aid has brought to the third world. One of Wright's entourage, a fellow Texan named Billy, reduced the matter to perhaps its crux: "You know, everything's alright to drank 'round heeah." Costa Rica is a Central American country where you can drink the water.

But in all fairness it meant more than that to Wright. As the day wound down he mused about the significance of the parade. He began with mechanical compliments: "Costa Rica is exemplary in many ways: the civility of the society, the glorification of education and democracy, and all those things that ennoble the human race." But suddenly his voice assumed a tone approaching wonder, "I felt so uplifted by that marvelously festive crowd, and I thought about how sad it is that we can't do that anymore in our country. Seeing the president just walk out of the church and into the crush of people and take to the streets was simply remarkable to me. It was a politician's dream!" It's a dream not possible in our country since the nightmare in Arlington, Texas, in November 1963, or perhaps since the ballroom of a Los Angeles hotel and the balcony of a Memphis motel in 1968.

Slowly the parade pushed onward, past low-rise, ramshackle San José, past street vendors selling apples from Washington State and big clusters of dark grapes, past bus stops and bars, fast food shops and pharmacies, camera stores, and clothing outlets, hotels and hardware stores. It rose with Avenida Dos, up a knoll from which one could see the city spread out below, and then, winding still upward, continued toward an imposing building that looked more like a fortress than a museum. Thick walls rose high above the earth, commanding a clear vista of the city.

This was the national museum, but the citadel aura was no personal figment: It had once been the national barracks, Fortress Bella Vista, until Don Pepe Figueres scaled its walls and pounded on the top with his sledgehammer, then took the keys that opened the big iron gate and handed them to one of his ministers with instructions that what had belonged to the army should now belong to the educators. Don Pepe was a master of symbolism, and the art has not been totally lost: As the parade approached, schoolchildren stood at the gate to welcome the dignitaries, having traded long-stemmed flowers for long-handled sledgehammers.

Inside the walls was a handsome rectangular courtyard displaying the ox carts that symbolize old Costa Rica, the national flowers in beds along walkways, and even a perfectly spherical ancient stone ball perhaps ten feet in diameter (one of many that exist around the country, although no archaeologist can ascertain why). Exhibits of Indian and Costa Rican artifacts and art, from gold orna-

ments to pottery to oil paintings, were arranged in cases
and on walls in the museum. For the festivities, a courtyard tent protected visitors from the intense sun, and in
an arched corridor open to the interior the dignitaries sat
at a long table.

The program indicated that Don Pepe would say a few
words, followed by President Arias. But Figueres did not
have the stamina to make his presentation, so it was up to
the president of the present, not the president of the past,
to make the address:

> Today marks thirty-nine years since those as-
> sembled, in this very place, the leaders of Costa
> Rica, accompanied by citizens who had arrived from
> every corner of the nation. Those who gathered here
> came to realize a simple and emotional ceremony.
> Those who gathered here reaffirmed that a history of
> peace can be built by men, when they have vision
> and courage. Those who gathered here came to ac-
> complish a unique act in the history of the world: To
> dissolve an army and to make Costa Rica a nation
> apart, a nation invincible.
>
> Today we meet again to mark thirty-nine years in
> the same place—then an army barracks, now a mu-
> seum—to remember and pay homage to those un-
> usual men and to give thanks to José Figueres
> Ferrer, the creator of our history of peace.
>
> Permit me to repeat the historic words which Don
> José Figueres spoke, the solemn pronouncement to
> our nation and to history. Hope to God that these
> words will be repeated every December first by
> every president of Costa Rica in the future. Hope to
> God that no generation forgets the courage and vi-

sion of those past, thanks to which our nation is special. Hope to God that we are able to transform the homages of today into a sacred tradition which we proudly celebrate year after year, to the abolition of the army.

Said José Figueres:

> The Regular Army of Costa Rica, which is the successor to the Army of National Liberation, surrenders the key to this barracks to the schools, for which to be converted into a center of culture.
>
> The Junta of the Second Republic officially declares the dissolution of the national army, because the security of our country is sufficiently protected by the police force.
>
> We firmly maintain the ideal of a new world in America. To that country of ideals of Washington, Lincoln, Bolívar, and Martí, we wish today to declare: "O, America! Other countries, your children also offer you their greatness. Little Costa Rica wants to offer forever, as now, along with its heart, its love of civility and democracy."

Costa Ricans silently appreciate this profound historical legacy, with a deep pride and satisfaction which we do not wish to hide. What did he give to us, our dear Don Pepe, with this decision? What are the differences for Costa Rica, having passed through a thirty-nine-year history without an army?

In these thirty-nine years, every country in Latin America has known a military dictatorship. Some exist today. Not Costa Rica. Our freedoms were never threatened; neither have we known oppression. The humiliation of a destiny governed by force and not by reason is unknown in Costa Rica.

11

In these thirty-nine years, all the countries of our America have seen the deaths of a young student, a farmer, a worker, in cruel and useless slaughter perpetrated by those stupid beasts in boots. In Costa Rica, no. Not a single mother has wept in our country over the death of someone by the dominance of a soldier, for the blindness of a tyrant.

In these thirty-nine years, thousands of Latin Americans have known exile, have suffered torture, imprisonment, and death at the hands of a dictator. In Costa Rica, no. Not one Costa Rican has left these lands and been unable to return freely. Nobody among us has known prison for expressing his ideas; not torture, much less death.

In these thirty-nine years, in which military barracks have been transformed into schools, our national symbol has been the teacher, who extols intelligence, and not the soldier, who crushed the people and who, even today, crushes people in other parts of the Americas.

In these thirty-nine years, the minorities of one extreme or another, who believe that they possess the absolute truth, have never tried to dominate by force of arms. For us, liberty is a permanent fact of life, and respect of elections is a part of our national spirit. For that reason, in our country nobody subscribes to a guerrilla or an armed force which intends to grab power to defend the interests and privileges of a minority. Our people know that extremists, no matter what kind, will never, never be able to violate these freedoms. Costa Rica is, truly, a unique nation on this earth, where the only weapons we know are the shared values of democracy, tolerance, peace, liberty, and solidarity.

The words were delivered evenly, without bluster, in a style more British than Latin. It was a speech designed to reinforce the fundamental shape of the Costa Rican national myth, that this is a nation with a deep respect for peace and individual rights.

Every country's identity is based in part on myths that spur it forward. It's a crucial element of nationalism. The United States is the Land of Opportunity, after all, and China is the Center of the World. In the Soviet Union Everyone Works, and in Cuba Everyone Eats. These myths create national pride as well as expectations; they become the yardsticks to gauge personal achievement and social success. Where myth and reality differ is the sociologist's turf, but basically if people believe the myth then they blame themselves when their lives don't measure up to it. When people no longer believe, then discontent runs deep.

What is so fascinating about the Costa Rican national mythology is that it is still so young, still in the process of being formed. George Washington and John Kennedy can share a stage. Just a few years ago, before Arias took office, no one celebrated December first as the anniversary of the abolition of the army; it is a holiday Arias has urged on the public. No doubt it will become ingrained, not only because Costa Ricans love holidays, but because it captures the emerging self-image so perfectly.

But nothing captured and enhanced that myth as well as the Nobel Peace Prize. It was an anointing for Costa Rica as much as for Arias. Just the sound of it, the 1987 Nobel Peace

Prize, set national bells ringing. It was the ultimate international recognition of the youthful national self-definition; it brought great vitality to the collective psyche of this little-noticed niche of the world. As Arias himself has said more than once since the announcement of the prize, "Now maybe people won't confuse us with Puerto Rico."

For Costa Rica, as everywhere, there are discrepancies between myth and fact, between real and ideal. Outsiders historically have seen Costa Rica as smaller than life and so have ignored its existence. But neither is Costa Rica larger than life, as inspirational as it can be at times.

This is no paradise after all. Yet surely it has a warm, accessible, civilized aspect. People kiss each other at the drop of a hat; they slip into affectionate diminutives of speech at the slightest provocation—and these are not superficial expressions; they spring from a deep reservoir of good intentions. Sometimes people take this trait for granted and refer to Costa Rica as the suburbia of Central America, the middle-class haven that everyone is supposed to aspire to but is shallow, empty at the core. Yes, they say, there is a polite stability and security, but where is the deep throb of Indian culture that beats through Guatemala, or the emotional heat that gives rise to the painters and poets of Nicaragua?

That attitude misses something crucial about Costa Rica, that its openness and inclusive charm may seem like nothing but veneer to people looking for heroes like Che, Fidel, and Sandino, but really is very hard to achieve and maintain. "I thought we were fighting to make a second Costa Rica," said a woman who had fought with the Sandinistas in Nicaragua, then became disillusioned and left her homeland and its revolution. "But it turned out we were fighting to make a second Cuba."

OF MYTHS AND MEN

The point was not lost on the U.S. congressional delegation. As Arias's speech ended, the crowd adjourned for a reception in the halls of the museum. The food was certainly straight out of the Suburban Reception Handbook: green olives and ham skewered with toothpicks; Ritz crackers with cheese spread; pastry cups filled with diced mushrooms; chopped herring; Coca-Cola and Fanta orange. The white wine was Costa Rican, however, and good enough to drink, as I talked with J. Wilson Morris, one of Jim Wright's key aides whose focus is Central America and who works with the steering and policy committee of the House Democratic membership. He is one of the myriad behind-the-scenes players in Washington, D.C., and might even qualify for the Costa Rican term *carpintero:* Like a carpenter, he puts shape to the words of the politicians, and sometimes the realization of the blueprint turns out to be what the carpenter chose to hammer into place.

I told him a bit of what I had been learning, about how intrigued I had become with this little multifaceted jewel of a country. In a dozen years as a journalist, I have covered small-town governments, national elections, and international conflict. But never, except maybe on the West Bank of Israel, had I felt that there was so much to be said that North Americans by and large had never heard before, so many false impressions to overcome and so much riding on a clearer understanding. I am no Central American expert, and maybe that is not so bad because "experts" are not the audience that I want to address about Costa Rica. If anything can excuse the hubris of a *gringo* journalist with barely passable Spanish who thinks he can write about the collective reality of a Central American country, it is only that the stakes are so high: United States foreign policy exerts life-and-death influence, and

15

ultimately that policy is the creation of gringo voters, like me, who pass judgment on the experts.

Morris seemed to understand what I was saying. Surveying the scene in progress, he spoke quietly yet with an underlying passion that would have been surprising only to those who had not yet experienced the authentic, civilized vitality of Costa Rica. "To let this country go down would be an incredible tragedy," he said. "It would be on the order of Cambodia. That's why I say screw the Nicaraguans, screw the contras, let's do what we can to protect Costa Rica."

Exactly the words Costa Ricans want to hear, exactly why the congressional delegations that seem to migrate south every month are always so welcome. A psychiatrist might call such policy positive rather than negative reinforcement, for the tendency is to support Arias and Costa Rica as well as criticize Ortega and Nicaragua. Then the psychiatrist might go on to wonder why such a big and powerful presence would need to feel so threatened by such a small, immature expression from Nicaragua.

Meanwhile, discussions over hors d'oeuvres were going every which way. Most of the U.S. embassy seemed to be around, including Dean Hinton, then the newly installed ambassador. He appeared to be more diplomatic than both Curtin Winsor, the ambassador twice removed who had said, "Nicaragua is like an infected piece of meat that attracts insects from all over," and Lewis Tambs, the ambassador once removed who reportedly told the CIA chief in Costa Rica that his only real mission as ambassador was to open a clandestine southern warfront against the Sandinistas.

This day, participants in the discussions were vice-presidents from four Central American countries, Venezuela's former president, and the vice-president of Spain. United

States congressmen, including Berman from California, Owens from Utah, Alexander from Arkansas, and Boehlert from New York, were mixing with the international press—when suddenly BOOM.

If a similar group had been gathered in any other country within a thousand miles, everyone would have hit the floor, machine guns would have bristled, and panic would have broken out, because it surely sounded as if some sort of weapon had just discharged. But this is Costa Rica, so instead, with an embarrassed laugh, a man reached down for a warm, shaken Coca-Cola bottle that had fallen and exploded. The conversation, which had lulled, resumed.

Then, to end the day's festivities, there was the mandatory press conference. Arias and Wright sat side by side before a thicket of microphones, answering alternately in Spanish and English. Both men were extremely cautious. Arias emphasized a tempered optimism with a plea for international goodwill to help move the peace process forward. Wright said: "It is right and proper that the peace plan for Central America be written by Central Americans and be carried out by Central Americans. Our role should not be to dictate terms, but be supportive of the process of peace." Given a full understanding of the United States' role in Central America over the decades, his sentiment was downright revolutionary.

When Arias was asked if the peace plan really could succeed, he answered grimly, "Now, more than ever, no one wants the war to go on. The war is incompatible with the future happiness of our children. . . . There must be peace. We cannot fail." Then, a smile beginning to appear, he shrugged his slightly hunched shoulders. *"Todo es posible,"* he concluded, eyes twinkling. All things are possible.

I found my attention turning to a tableau near the door. A small old man sat in a chair surrounded by a cluster of young people, holding a glass of Coke in his hand. His gray-blue eyes seemed to lose their focus momentarily, then sharpen. I tried to imagine what might be going through his mind, how different this place must have looked thirty-nine years ago. Then death had been in the air, not pleasantries. The room had held weapons, not historical exhibits.

This man, watching dignitaries of the hemisphere chitchat, had been exiled in the 1940s for daring to speak out against his government, then returned to fight against that very government because it had refused to accept the verdict of a national election. Several thousand people had died in the battles, as heavy a percentage of casualties for Costa Rica as our Civil War inflicted on us. Don Pepe Figueres faced down two more invasions from Nicaraguan-based forces in the following months and years, both times without the benefit of a standing army. He created what democracy needed: time to root deeply in the national soil.

Here was the man who idolized Franklin Roosevelt, nationalized the banks, and institutionalized Social Security, universal suffrage, a minimum wage, and tax aimed at the rich—while at the same time sending arms to help Castro win his revolution and encouraging efforts to overthrow Nicaragua's dictator, Somoza, whom FDR referred to in a famous line as "a son of a bitch, but our son of a bitch."

So Arias, leading Costa Rica along an international tightrope, certainly has had quite an act to follow—and study. As with most family members, political or otherwise, the relationship between him and Figueres has not always been warm and easy, although it has been intimate. Indeed, as much as Oscar Arias owes his political career to José Figueres, he owes his presidency to his own willingness to

18

break away from the old generation, the "Generation of 1948." He represents a new consensus and a revival of spirit. In my travels and interviews across the country, it was startling to realize how well this young president suits his nation—and how no one dreamed the fit would be this good until literally the moment he took office.

How do you even begin to explain all this? How do you explain a phenomenon like the Arias presidency without first explaining the Figueres revolution that made Arias possible? How do you explain the Figueres revolution independently of the national persona, a collective consciousness far deeper than politics that made a revolution like Figueres's possible? And how do you explain a national character that defines the Arias presidency even as it is being changed by the Arias presidency?

It's one of those Catch-22s, I thought, watching Don Pepe struggle to his feet, watching younger hands gently keep him erect and take the glass of Coca-Cola, watching this small old man helped to his car at the end of the day of the first of December. It's the historian's constant question: Does a society create its people or do the people create the society?

The answer, as always, is both ways to the middle. But as fascinating and complex as today's political characters can be, their parade is only the latest of many to march across this extraordinary little country the size of West Virginia, home to 2.5 million people, a place that Columbus named Costa Rica.

CHAPTER TWO

South of the Border

As it turned out, Columbus called the place Costa Rica, or Rich Coast, for all the wrong reasons. When the great explorer blew ashore on his fourth and final trip to the Americas in 1502, he came to rest in a bay at an Indian village called Cariari, which roughly translates as *eagle's head* and was interpreted to be the title for the head of the tribe as well. Columbus saw natives on the shore, many of whom wore gold eagles on chains around their necks. It was that same gleam of gold that would drive Spaniards throughout the Americas wild and incite them to destroy ancient civilizations.

To satisfy his sponsors, Columbus needed to be part journalist. He asked his key question and was told that there was plenty more of the shiny stuff not far away. His sources were bad and the stories gross exaggerations, but they fueled mad quests for centuries to come and gave Costa Rica its name. It was only the first of many ironic misunderstandings.

The Indians were peaceful, interested in trade. Columbus's crew responded by kidnapping two men to serve as guides along the treacherous coastal waterways. It was hardly a way to make friends, and Columbus himself apparently had some misgivings about the ill will it caused, but he felt he had no choice. He was not a settler, after all, and only a journalist by necessity. He was an explorer. Those who followed in his wake would have to deal with the animosity of the Indians, whose feelings the *conquistadores* never cared too much about anyway.

As it turned out, the Spanish got both a lot more and a lot less than they bargained for from the Indians who lived in Costa Rica. At the time of the Spanish "discovery," the total population was reported to have been around twenty-seven thousand, divided into five tribes: the Corobica, Boruca, Chorotega, Nahua, and Carib. Some historians say that of these, the Corobici were the most ancient and developed. Others say it was the Chorotega. Whichever, a major center of culture had been established along the Gulf of Nicoya in what is now the middle of Costa Rica. Large temples and markets existed, the cacao bean served as the local currency, and society was so far advanced that people even practiced counterfeiting, carefully emptying the beans of their powder, refilling them with earth, and trading once more. Missionaries got right to work, and by the 1520s there already were reports that as many as six thousand Indians had been baptized.

The main interest most Spaniards had in the Indians

was not their souls, however, but their bodies. They wanted slaves. Yet the Costa Ricans thwarted that desire, and to this day Costa Rican democracy owes the ancient Indian tribes a huge debt. Unlike the Aztecs or Mayans, the native Costa Ricans were decentralized and fiercely independent. In other parts of Central America the Spaniards could lop off the head of the tribal ruler and expect much of the population to fall into submission. In Costa Rica, each time they thought they had reached the head, they found, like Hercules with the Hydra, not one but many. A built-in force of Indian slaves working giant plantations ruled by tiny, repressive oligarchies was not possible. However, this was not what most Spaniards bargained for; a full century after Columbus's discovery, only six hundred Spaniards lived in Costa Rica.

The geography also played a role in Costa Rica's resistance to Spanish settlement. A ring of rugged mountains and volcanoes isolated the country's Central Plateau. The regional capital of Spanish government was in Guatemala; in many ways it might as well have been in Madrid. Without much gold, without wide-open fertile plains for centralized farming (hence wealth and taxes), those who chose to stick it out in Costa Rica were left much to their own devices.

There was some slavery, and there were revolts. The Indian civilization was wiped out by war and disease, except for those who retreated deep into the wild Talamanca Mountains of southeast Costa Rica, repulsed the Spanish conquistadores with greater valor than any other nation of the Indies, according to one historian, and today still cling barely to a semblance of their old life.

But by and large the Spaniards who made it in Costa Rica could not be conquistadores. They had to become *campesinos* instead, small farmers who got their hands and boots dirty subsisting on their own land. In the next century, far to the north, Thomas Jefferson would talk and dream about how the independent landowner, the small farmer, could become the backbone and ballast of true democracy. In Costa Rica, midwifed by poverty, geography, and luck, a form of Jeffersonian democracy was already being born.

But it was a long, difficult labor. The early 1700s were a low point. The old capital, Cartago, once called Veragua, had been established as far back as 1563 but still consisted of nothing more than seventy adobe huts and one church. In 1723 the nearby volcano, Irazu, blew its top (as it still periodically blows), and the place was destroyed.

Cartago's sparseness before its ruin was symbolic of the general run of things. As late as 1821, Costa Rica had a population of only fifty-seven thousand, including remote Indian villages. One effect of a low labor supply was that field hands on farms and cowboys on the open cattle ranches of Guanacaste Province were far from slaves: employees were in demand, so they were paid wages and often could choose whom to work for. It may have been cheaper that way for the employers, but it certainly was freer for the working people.

Eighteen twenty-one was a turning point for Central America, and once again Costa Rica's backwater status saved it from much of the turmoil and exploitation that wracked the rest of the region. At long last the inevitable had happened: First Mexico and then all of the Central American colonies were granted independence from Spain. But instead of joining Mexico in a new empire, Central Americans merged forces and created a nation of their own that appropriately enough was called the Central American Empire. It was not a long-lived historical expression, gone from the face of the earth by 1839.

In Costa Rica, the idea was dispensed with even earlier. In 1835 a civil war was fought over annexation to this new Central American nation, the main result of which was that the "Republicans" of the time won, moved the national capital from Cartago to San José, and managed to cling to Costa Rican nationalism until the rest of the region accepted the inevitable and splintered roughly into the nations we know today.

Over the next sixty-five years, Costa Rica's political history would belie its myth of a peacefully evolving democracy. From 1824 through 1870 twenty-two men held power in the country for three months or more. In 1870 Costa Rica's first real military "strong man," Tomás Guardia, assumed power in a coup and ruled until 1882. His brother-in-law took over after him, followed by the brother-in-law's son-in-law. The family affair lasted through 1889, when what is generally accepted as Costa Rica's first true election took place. From the 1830s until the turn of the century the military, in some form or other, was in power at least half of the time, a third or more of the presidents resigned before completing their terms, and one in five was the victim of some form of coup.

Even more significant, nearly all of these generals turned out to be a part of the new elite, the coffee-growing aristocracy. Coffee arrived in Costa Rica from Jamaica, in 1808, as a ship captain's gift to the local governor. By the 1840s it had adopted its new home with a vengeance. The bean which most of the world would hate to do without had changed Costa Rica forever, blanketing the hillsides with its rich green leaves, encouraging both the formation of the first Costa Rican aristocracy and a higher standard of living for thousands of families who would own small *fincas*, coffee plots on land near their homes.

Although land and wealth slowly began to centralize and pyramid, most campesinos were not pressured to sell out to land barons. Instead, the big players tended to control the distribution, serving as middlemen to whom all the little growers brought their harvest, willing buyers from willing sellers. The Jeffersonian ideal was being violated, and yet most Costa Ricans did not feel oppressed and usurped. No doubt there was exploitation, but in comparison to the rest of Central America it took as benign a form as exploitation can. Control and manipulation were more subtle, more accepted. It never got to the same point as in Guatemala, for example, where the president of the 1870s, Justo Rufino Barrios, picked up a horsewhip and said, "This is the constitution I govern by."

It is this benign aspect of Costa Rican history that is difficult to grasp, let alone explain. Yes, there was war and pestilence, a greedy multinational corporation that appeared in the form of United Fruit, an aristocracy that looked out for itself, a military that tended to seize power at opportune moments—all the sources of tears and bitterness that too many third world countries know too well. But the abuse never bloomed into barbarity. There were built-in checks and balances in the national character, more than in the national government, that seemed to kick in at crucial moments. A military strongman like Guardia would not be remembered for his oppression, but rather for setting up at least the trappings of a democratic constitution and building a railroad. His nephew-in-law would be remembered not as the feeble second generation of a dynasty, but as the man who established public education and organized free elections.

There are many theories about why this fundamental decency crept into Costa Rican society and stayed there. The Jeffersonian small-landowner ideal is one: There was a solid block of self-made *hombres* in the middle of the country who were not easily moved and who had no truck with oppression. It is also true that many of the Spaniards who came to Costa Rica traced roots back through eras of persecution themselves: Many were from Sephardic Jewish families who had converted to Roman Catholicism during the Spanish Inquisition but, even so, left in search of cleaner air to breathe.

Indeed, as powerful and dominant as the Roman Catholic church has been in Costa Rica, it is less powerful and less dominant than in most any other country in Latin America. There was a tension and interplay between government and religion that tended to work in favor of a growing middle class, tended to encourage reform and liberalism. The coffee barons wanted a counterweight to the church, which encouraged a government that did more than throw a few sacks of beans to the masses.

Then there is the unfortunate argument that rears its ugly head too often in places like *sodas* (the Costa Rican word for a small bar or food joint), where amateur social analysts trade insights. It might take a *cerveza* or two, but sooner or later someone will say, "After all, the plain truth is that Costa Ricans are white." It's one of those insidious arguments that has just enough basis in fact so that someone who wants to be racist can find evidence to support the feeling. Of course, what Costa Ricans consider "white," Minnesotans would call "Chicano." And *mestizos*, people of mixed heritage, comprise a large percentage of the population. But at least in the area of the Central Plateau, where most people live, there is an unusual sense of homogeneity. Beyond the Central Plateau the stereotype breaks down completely: In Guanacaste, people tend to look darker, more like Nicaraguans, whereas along the Atlantic Coast, around the city of Limón, not only are people black-skinned, but they speak a Caribbean English as much as Spanish. The reason for that, as we will see, is a story unto itself.

But getting back to the benign character of Costa Rican history, one more important ingredient has to be added to the stew: Unlike most every other nation of the region, at no time has Costa Rica been invaded and occupied by United States forces. It is not a pleasant bit of history for gringos to consider, and many tend to overlook it, but we do flex our muscles south, be it as a major land-grab from Mexico, a quick expedition to Grenada, an invasion of the Dominican Republic or Cuba, an occupation of El Salvador or Nicaragua, or even an assassination in Chile. These things have happened regularly over the past century and a half and they can inflict profound damage on the national psyche of a small country.

Costa Rica never had to suffer that kind of shame. Indeed, the story of the only time Costa Rica had to fight an armed invader from the United States is an exalted moment in the schoolbooks and gave rise to the country's only national war hero (who turned out to be a peasant drummer boy). For drama and Costa Rican flavor, it is a tale worth telling.

The year was 1856, and there were big doings in the northern part of the hemisphere. Slavery was the burning question of the day, but other things were on people's minds as well. For example, Cornelius Vanderbilt was

27

thinking about how much money there was to be made by transporting various items to the gold-rush towns springing up in the West—not to mention the global trading advantages of connecting the Atlantic and Pacific oceans without having to steam all the way down past the wild tip of South America. A canal, Vanderbilt reasoned, could make a rich man yet richer. And a logical place, he figured, was where Nicaragua meets Costa Rica, because the San Juan River and Lake Nicaragua take care of a lot of the digging, leaving only eighteen dry miles to complete a waterway to the Pacific. With Manifest Destiny in the air and James Buchanan about to become president, it didn't seem like an impossible dream.

The point man for this scheme turned out to be William Walker, one of history's unlikely business partners. Walker was a physical shrimp, not much past five feet and a hundred pounds, apparently a brilliant student who studied both law and medicine and graduated with degrees while still a teenager. Then his life took a strange twist, leading him to the gold mines of California, into journalism, and finally into mercenary wars. He became a filibuster, not in the sense of delivering drawn-out speeches in the halls of Congress, but of a private military adventurer in a foreign country. By the 1850s he had already proclaimed himself the president of part of northern Mexico, although the Mexican army took exception and chased him back to the United States, where his notoriety grew.

The money behind Walker and his men seemed to be a group called the Knights of the Golden Circle, whose purpose was to promote slavery. This was in keeping with a strong school of thought in the United States that suggested that Mexico and Central America could become territories where slavery was allowed. Walker not only appealed to this group, but proposed making the location of his next foray Nicaragua, so Cornelius Vanderbilt and company might also find reason to be pleased. And with pleasure comes money.

In June 1855, Walker landed in Nicaragua with a force described as anywhere from fifty-eight to one hundred sixty-five filibusters. He descended on a nation in turmoil, split among political factions, one of which opened the door to Walker by signing a decree that welcomed new settlers into the country. Walker never did settle down, but with the help of more reinforcements from California and the most advanced carbines and pistols of the day, he managed to seize control of the government of Nicaragua. Those were the days when no one quibbled about words like *contra* or *freedom fighter*; Walker went right ahead and called himself both President of Nicaragua and Chief General of the Army.

Walker had his toehold, but, as far as both the slavery and canal interests behind him were concerned, this was only the beginning. The next logical step was to move south to make sure that both shores of the future canal were secure and to topple the next domino. Seeing a smaller, more docile country, with even less of a standing armed force than Nicaragua, Walker apparently assumed that Costa Rica wouldn't be much of a problem.

The Costa Ricans saw him coming, which was part of what saved them. The president at the time was Juan Rafael Mora, and on November 20, 1855, he delivered what might be called a classic Costa Rican call to arms. In Spanish, the crux of it was: "*¡Alerta, costarricenses! No interrumpáis vuestras nobles faenas, pero preparad vuestras armas.*" In rough translation, with the flowery rhetoric removed, what he said was, "Hey, Costa Ricans, don't stop what you're doing, but we're about to have a war on our hands."

It took almost four months, but Mora was right. In March 1856, according to Costa Rican history books, Walker's Nicaragua declared war on Costa Rica. By the sixteenth of the month, a band of three hundred to four hundred seasoned filibusters, led by Walker's friend Louis Schlessinger, crossed the border headed toward San José.

What they couldn't have known was that almost two weeks earlier Mora had begun mobilizing a force to beat them back. There was was scarcely a soldier among this Costa Rican army, which was composed of farmers and merchants carrying anything from machetes and swords to old blunderbuss guns that needed to be stuffed, filled with shot and ball, and lit by a flint before every firing. But thousands left San José to fight, and although thousands of the thousands dropped by the wayside during the long, hard march north toward Nicaragua, a few thousand were left when the filibusters were located. At the head of the rag-tag troop was the brother of the president, General José Joaquín Mora.

The scene of the battle was Santa Rosa, an old hacienda about twenty miles south of the border along what is now the Pan-American Highway. One of the oldest and biggest cattle ranches in the country, Santa Rosa had been in operation since the late 1560s. The building itself is a handsome Spanish structure with red clay half-pipe roofing, white stucco walls, a wraparound covered porch, stables, a courtyard garden, and a simple interior dominated by dark wood floor and beams. (It would serve as a perfect set for an old Zorro movie.) And it was only natural that the filibusters would stop there to rest and regroup.

On the afternoon of March 20, the battle was joined. Walker's men were arrayed around the stout walls of the hacienda house, surrounded by Costa Ricans. The best surviving account of what happened next is in the report that General Mora made shortly thereafter to his brother, President Mora:

> When everything was ready, I ordered the columns of soldiers to form at the end of the land. At the sound of the blasts of the bugles, our soldiers all ran to the position that had been indicated.
> The filibusters did not fire one shot; they waited for us close by with the hope that their first volley would defeat us. Neither did our troops fire until they were about twenty varas [roughly sixty-five feet] from the enemy. Then a sustained volley broke out that lasted until the Costa Ricans reached the fences. From that moment on only the pirates fired. Our soldiers jumped into the corrals unrestrained by the devastating barrage directed towards them.
> Here is where the valiant official Manuel Rojas was killed. Once inside there was no hope for the renegades. Sabers and bayonets ripped them to pieces and, terrorized, they were not able to even fire their guns.
> In this way they were beaten back to the house where they locked themselves in at the same time that Captain Gutiérrez's men, having taken possession of the hill, surrounded them. It was then Captain Manuel Quiros died. He was wounded by jumping the fence into the patio. His last words were directed to his soldiers in arms: "Go on," he said. . . .
> I gave the order for the cavalry to attack as it seemed to me that the moment to run the filibusters

out of their lair was almost at hand. But on seeing that it was not time yet, we marched to the hill in front and waited for the right moment.

All this occurred in five minutes. Soon the artillery was sent into action: Captain Marin fired his cannons against the front and right-hand side of the house, opening several breaches. But this only served to inflame the desperadoes more and they sent back heavier fire.

Impatiently and at the risk of becoming a target for the enemy, Colonel Salazar came running to ask me if, in order to protect his men, he could set fire to the house of a Costa Rican landowner. Worried on seeing him come towards me and fearing that he might be wounded, I went forward to meet him and gave him permission to carry out his request. He returned to give the order to his soldiers who received it with joyous shouts. However, there was not enough time. Valiant Captain Gutiérrez, forgetting the orders he had, entered the grounds and, rushing forward to a stable that had been fortified and was bristling with rifles, with his saber in one hand and his pistol in the other, met a painful and premature death. The fury that his death caused among the troops was so great that nothing could restrain them. The house was invaded on all sides and the filibusters, on finding a way out over the hill which the unsuccessful Gutiérrez was supposed to cover, fled in a mad rush. Although they were pursued and cut down on all sides, many managed to escape.[1]

It is a fascinating account for what it says, what it implies, and what it doesn't say. It says that these valiant amateurs at war used their numbers and bravery to rout the invaders, worrying even as they fought about the damage they were doing to Costa Rican property. It implies that General Mora didn't have very good control of the troops: He ordered a calvary attack that never happened and, because "valiant Captain Gutiérrez" wouldn't follow orders and maintain his position, he not only died but many of the filibusters escaped. What it doesn't say is that this most famous of Costa Rican battles probably resulted in fewer than fifty deaths. The entire length of battle, as General Mora carefully timed it, was fourteen minutes.

But the fighting was not over. The Costa Ricans chased Walker's men north, hounding them back to the border and beyond. Three weeks later, on April 11, 1856, in the Nicaraguan town of Rivas, battle was pitched again. Once more, the filibusters were surrounded, protected by a sturdy wooden building that could not be pierced. Once more, the solution seemed to be to set the place on fire, (one story has it that, in fine Costa Rican fashion, the troops voted on the question). This time, however, there were no prematurely valiant captains messing things up. Instead, there was Juan Santamaría.

As legend has it, Juan Santamaría was a former sacristan from the city of Alajuela; if he was as good a keeper of the sacred vessels of the church as he has been a keeper of the symbol of the sacred national honor, then he must have been quite a competent youngster. He joined the army as nothing more than than a drummer boy, presumably keeping the beat as the troops marched farther and farther north. And when the fateful battle of Rivas took place, it was Juan Santamaría who volunteered to approach the

33

barricaded filibusters with a torch in hand and set fire to the building.

Now a few wags have implied over the years that Juan might not exactly have volunteered—that the might have *been* volunteered—but no doubt they are nothing more than cynics who derive satisfaction from popping national balloons. Because, as the story goes, Juan first approached the dangerous building, managed to get his torch in place, and escaped without injury, only to find that the fire did not catch. And so, beyond any call of duty or vicarious volunteerism, Juan Santamaría returned with another torch in hand as well as some petroleum to help things along. This time he was shot in his upraised arm as he approached, but even that didn't stop him—he switched the flame to the other hand and kept coming. He reached the building, finally torching it with enough competence to drive the miscreants out, and then fell to his death in a hail of gunfire.

As the story spread, the kid from Alajuela became a national hero to the Costa Ricans' liking: A simple, small drummer boy who had as much courage as filibustering North Americans and who understood what it meant to rise to an occasion. They remember him every April 11.

Even such heroism was not the end of Walker. He escaped and hung in there for another year, until it became clear that neither slavery nor a canal was an immediate reality. President Buchanan was unhappy about the former, while Cornelius Vanderbilt felt betrayed about the latter (and before long funded the Costa Rican resistance). Walker soon knew what it felt like to have his two legs cut out from under, and after various machinations inspired by delusions of grandeur, he was shot and killed in Honduras in 1860. Etched on his tombstone are said to be these words: "Glory to the patriots who freed Central America of such a bloody pirate! Curses to those who brought him and to those who helped him."

Yet the end of Walker was not the end of the short war's effects. General Mora should have returned a triumphant hero, but instead he and his soldiers brought cholera back to Costa Rica along with victory, and the plague killed more than ten thousand people before it was done, a full tenth of the population. The slaughter exceeded anything a blunderbuss or saber could have accomplished, and when the Moras tried to manipulate the ensuing election to assure their stay in power, they were overthrown. Not long after, the general tried to retake the government by coup, lost the struggle, and wound up facing a firing squad in San Salvador in December 1860. It would be almost a century before the Mora name was resurrected to hero status, celebrating the opposition to armed imperialism.

Actually, in the Costa Rican consciousness the name Santa Rosa carries many more valiant connotations than the name Mora. It was at this same hacienda in 1919 that the first battle to overthrow one of the few truly repressive Costa Rican dictators, General Federico Tinoco, was fought. And yet again, in 1955, at Santa Rosa, then-President Don Pepe Figueres's rural guard battled an armed force trying to remove his elected government from power. In recognition of all this historical significance, Santa Rosa is now the center of a sprawling national park. The hacienda house remains intact, the stables have been converted to a small museum, and the hill where Captain Gutiérrez refused to cool his heels is the site of a tall national monument dedicated to the heroes from 1856 through 1955. Eight names are honored from the 1955 skirmish; it gave me particular pleasure that two of them are journalists'.

Finally, Santa Rosa is noted for one more historical event. It was on land since incorporated into the expanding national park around the hacienda that, in 1985, a mysterious Panamanian corporation built a mile-long airstrip in the middle of nowhere. It seemed that this "Udall Corporation" was a creation, in part, of a fellow who worked in the basement of the White House by the name of Oliver North. It turned out that this airstrip, code named "Point West" (not to be confused with West Point) was used in "Project Democracy" to direct secret and illegal resupply efforts to the Nicaraguan contras from July 1985 through February 1986, as well as acting "as the primary abort base for aircraft damaged by Sandinista anti-aircraft fire," according to a memo of Oliver North's included in the Tower Commission Report on the Iran-contra affair. And as anyone who lives near Santa Rosa can attest, when U.S. Undersecretary of State Elliott Abrams testified in Washington that, "My understanding was nobody ever used the airstrip,"[2] he was either misinformed or lying.

Most likely he was lying. Otherwise how can you explain the Tower Commission's finding that Abrams participated in a blackmail of the newly elected president of Costa Rica, Oscar Arias, in which he threatened to withhold United States foreign aid if Arias revealed the existence of the secret airstrip? Its existence was not immediately revealed, but it was quickly shut down by the Arias government, well before the Costa Rican press exposed the facts.

So there is quite a spotlight on Santa Rosa, quite a focus on what is nothing more than a big, old hacienda in

Guanacaste Province. But this long sequence of dramatic events is no mere coincidence. Costa Rican history tends to originate in the north, be it the immediate north of Nicaragua or the far north of the United States. The people who make it into the history books tend to descend on Costa Rica, which means that Costa Ricans tend to head north to meet them. Santa Rosa, a day's march from the Nicaraguan border along the Pan-American highway, is where history goes through customs.

In this generation, Oliver North notwithstanding, things have changed a bit. The news still tends to come from the north, but passengers in jets fly over Santa Rosa. They arrive directly in San José and pass through customs at the Juan Santamaría International Airport.

CHAPTER THREE

Bright Lights, Big City

Depending on where you came from, and where you're coming from, stepping past customs at the Juan Santamaría International Airport can be anything from a mundane to a shocking experience. If the reference point is Miami, then the airport certainly is no big deal. You can walk out the door into a cluster of taxis—mostly spiffy Toyotas—whose hustling drivers are looking for fares, and for ten bucks you get a twenty-five-minute ride downtown. Or you can walk over to one of the seven car-rental booths across the street, choose from Hertz or Avis, Ada or Santos, and for around thirty-five dollars drive wherever you feel like driving. *No problema*. Maybe a young guy like Ephraim Arias at Budget Rental will take care of you competently, with good English, and if you make a reservation beforehand, he actually might know you're coming. Is Ephraim related to the president? "If I was related to the president," he asked, "would I be working in a car-rental place?"

If the reference point is Managua, Nicaragua, where daily flights shuttle to and fro, then the airport takes on another reality. In Managua, cabs (when you find one) are usually old jalopies. Rental cars? Virtually impossible to find. There are no big new cars, no fancy taxis at anyone's beck and call. Blame it on the contras, or blame it on the Sandinistas, but either way the shock of the difference makes Nicaraguans see Costa Rican life as yet another notch higher than their own. Costa Ricans know it, maybe too well; their often repeated, nearly smug aphorism is, "What's the only propaganda we need for our way of life? Send a Costa Rican to Nicaragua for a week."

The border is only about two hundred fifty kilometers north, as the road sign at the airport exit says, but to get to San José you turn the other way and jump on the big *autopista* headed east. Within that twenty-five-minute ride, crammed along the road to the nation's capital, is a parade of images that present a quick and accurate sense of the country. Below flashy billboards advertising everything from cigarettes to cars to Kentucky Fried Chicken and Coca-Cola is a combination of industrial factories, large-scale growing operations for ornamental plants and flowers, and even coffee plots tucked among modernity, still subsisting in the shade of banana trees. Ramshackle, crumbled houses on the hill were erected by a group of poor people who occupied that land, the most visible spot they could find, and banged together a squatters ghetto.

They figured they could embarrass the government into finding them better housing. They were right.

Unlike in the rest of Central America, few people walk along the shoulders of the highway with heavy bundles of possessions or produce for market. More common are ten-speed bicyclists with fancy helmets and skin-tight black racing pants who speed along the breakdown lane—although breathing the diesel exhaust blasting out of the Mercedes and Volvo buses must be the equivalent of smoking a few packs of cigarettes a day.

The people who are on the side of the road are waiting, carefully lined up, at bus stops. They are well dressed, and many carry newspapers under their arms. The country has had free and compulsory education of some form since 1869, and the literacy rate is said to be near 90 percent (although a third-grade education qualifies as "literate"). The country, small as it is, supports five newspapers and a handful of magazines and guides. The biggest paper, *La Nación,* has a circulation of seventy thousand, which means it is bought by almost 3 percent of the entire population of Costa Rica.

There is one stoplight on the highway between the airport and the city, and it is a node of commerce, particularly for hawkers of lottery tickets. There's a big yellow electric totem pole of a sign announcing La Cariari. It has nothing to do with Columbus or Indians—it's the sign of the posh hotel where everyone from Ronald Reagan, George Shultz, Jimmy Carter, and Henry Kissinger to Jimmy Connors, Warren Beatty, Bud Grant, and Colonel Harland Sanders has visited, as the photos on the wall will prove.

A few miles closer to town is the old toll booth where collectors used to create monster traffic jams in order to

collect seven *colones*, about a dime per car, which probably wasted at least that much in gas. They got rid of the
toll and now use the place to stop and ticket speeders.
Silencio, commands a road sign; there's a hospital nearby,
so lay off the horn.

On the hillside above, a white-steepled church catches
the sun and gleams, while above even that, mysterious
blue mountains ring San José, their crowns often veiled in
clouds that cascade down in the late afternoon for a
shower and then return to their heights.

Past the Hotel Corbici (Why is it that people name
things for the places and cultures they've destroyed?) and
past the Hotel Irazu (Now there's a twist—the volcano
Irazu could destroy San José, not the other way around) is
the largest park of San José, called La Sabana, which
opens out on the right behind the Costa Rican Museum of
Art. The museum used to be an airport terminal before
Juan Santamaría took over.

The Sabana is a huge, multifaceted open space, and on
a typical Sunday afternoon a dozen soccer games of vary-
ing degrees of professionalism can be in progress at once
with plenty of room to spare for a few softball, basketball,
and tennis games, bicycle gangs streaming along path-
ways, lovers clinging to each other under the pine trees,
families picnicking on the grass, not to mention a Chris-
tian revival meeting with hundreds swaying and singing to
Spanish gospel. *"Cristo para mí,"* people shout (Christ for
me).

Inside the museum, which has an admission charge of
seven cents, the evocative work of one of Costa Rica's in-
ternationally celebrated artists, Francisco Amighetti, fills
the walls. Early landscapes painted near Taos, New Mexico, in the 1930s and 1940s are straightforward, colorful.

His frescoes mounted on public walls around Costa Rica, which were created at the time of the 1948 revolution, are full of epic symbols of Mother Earth: corn planted and harvested, sugarcane leveled with machetes, women and children running from soldiers with guns. There are also more recent prints and woodcuts, which the Japanese much admire, whose images are less heroic, more personal and abstract.

"I was always escaping from here," said Amighetti, now more than eighty years old, talking about his earlier years of travel, as he sat in his handsome small apartment at the edge of the city. "But I was also finding that Costa Rica *is* all the other places. There is only one man and woman everywhere. And I can't jump over my own shadow, so I create about myself."

These are the sentiments of a universal humanist, but one with a pragmatic national flair that led him to teach for more than twenty years as well as create. As his students passed by, semester after semester, Amighetti found that many of the images that lingered with him were those he had seen when he was barely twenty years old: a country man approaching the city of San José, walking with a machete in his hand and a sombrero on his head. Or a pair of oxen, yoked in heavy wood, pulling a loaded cart resting on wooden wheels.

Faced with what San José has become, Amighetti refers to his memories as "souvenirs, nostalgia," but the words are not meant to dismiss their importance. "If you see my mural in the airport," he continues, "behind Juan Santamaría, you see the rhythm of life in Costa Rica. So if the struggle has any reason, it's so that the peasants, the farmers, the people can continue the pastoral sense of Costa Rican life."

As Amighetti has grown older, and as San José has grown less pastoral, the artist's work has become darker. Mythic panoramas have been replaced by depictions of taverns where men sit depressed and drunk. Amighetti does not refer to this as social commentary, yet his stature is such that his vision has to be seen as cultural. After all, this is an artist who offered as a public manifesto the following thoughts to his colleagues:

> The painter who wishes to feel integrated in the community, to be considered as useful and necessary as a mason, or carpenter, cannot service only an idle group which considers the enjoyment of art to be some leisurely, nice pastime and a luxury of the spirit; rather, he must make contact with people in every walk of life, and assimilate those actions with the art in the measure of his capabilities.

The measure of San José's capabilities is found on the *avenidas* and *calles*, the avenues and cross streets that make an urban grid. This is not a pretty city, an old city, or even a Spanish city. About ten years ago people gave up trying to keep all the street signs in Spanish, accepting *Parqueo* (parking) for *Estacionar*. Now a look down the street shows the likes of Archi's Fried Chicken, McDonald's, and Billy Boy Hamburgers more often than a Cerrajeria (locksmith), Niñerias (children's clothes store), or Tienda Regis (lingerie store). In fact, when people give directions around San José, they very often say things like, "Go to the second Kentucky Fried Chicken, and take a left."

San José is the national hub, the capital and center of Costa Rica. A good 660,000 people live here, 30 percent of the nation. It is a magnet drawing Costa Ricans with dreams of opportunity. To do business in the country, you have to come to San José. To be a politician of stature, you have to come to San José. To travel, to bank, to become any kind of a big fish in the small pond, you have to come to San José. Possessed of its own tempo and value, the city has become so modern so quickly that now there is a saying: "Outside of San José, there is a country called Costa Rica."

The turmoil of the city is not overpowering by gringo standards, although the streets clog with traffic and the sidewalks fill with pedestrians. But if one comes from the provinces, where small, ordered village centers are always clustered around a park and a church, where men tip their hats and people stop to chat, where pickpockets are unknown, the city can be overwhelmingly impersonal. No longer do you see Amighetti's man in a sombrero with a machete making his way; men move in suits and carry briefcases. A team of oxen would be as out of place here as in San Diego. Yet sometimes still a caballero, a lean man more at home on horseback, wearing his best cowboy hat, will stop at a streetcorner and look around, trying to fig-ure out which way to turn to get to the bank.

Even though the streets have a logical odd-and-even numbering pattern, a visitor can be excused for becoming disoriented. There are few dramatic landmarks: the archi-tecture is repetitive and pretty much nondescript—not many high rises have found their way to San José. Few public parks break up the bustle, though people make good use of them. Take the *oreros* for example, the gold panners who work up in the mountains, still sifting and digging for the elusive gleam. When they thought the government had given them a bum deal over a dispute about access to land, they moved into a park and lived there for a few weeks until a settlement was negotiated. In Costa Rica if you want to get something done, go to San José.

In the middle of all this sits the National Theater, one of the few buildings that predates this century. Supposedly a crown jewel of national pride and architecture, its history actually connotes something a little different. The building was erected in the 1890s, funded by the burgeoning coffee barons who apparently felt embarrassed and slighted when a lovely prima donna of the time would not come from Guatemala to perform because there was no suitable theater to receive her. By 1897 the theater was ready, its hall a scaled-down version of the Paris Opera House, its architecture, art, and materials in every way derivative of European examples. It is beautiful, but Costa Rican only because it is miniature.

In many ways, people make better use of the open space around the theater than they do of the theater itself. Vendors set up portable wagons to sell leather work produced in cooperative shops in the small town of Sarchi, or rope hammocks, bead necklaces, and small clay animals that double as flutes. Around the corner an enterprising comedian might practice his stand-up routine. Or an impromptu preacher might fill the air with dire predictions, thumping a Bible against his head between phrases, prompting giggles from teenagers.

What really powers and defines San Josés's street life is commerce. Avenida Central, which splits the downtown in half, proves that Costa Ricans are among the world's ultimate consumers. They are willing to work two or three jobs to keep up with their various installment payments, willing to shoulder the largest per capita debt in Central America as long as the Rayban sunglasses, Sony Walkmans, Calvin Klein jeans, and Motorola television sets stay within reach. From block to block the variety of goods is astonishing, rivaling a side street in New York City: Store after store is dedicated to shirts, jewelry, toys, watches, fabrics, pants, boom boxes, silverware, belts, crystal, gold, dresses, baby clothes, lingerie, shoes. Yet even in the cheapest outlets, a pair of pants for a teenage girl costs 1,043 colones (roughly $15.50), while a basic shirt might go for about $8.00. Most of the toys are made in Taiwan. The handmade native Costa Rican garments are usually exported for sale in United States boutiques.

At Christmastime, things really get rolling *tico* style. Christmas is a national holiday that lasts the good part of a month, dedicated to God, yes, but also to the affairs of man. The wheels of government basically halt, most commerce outside of the buying and selling of Christmas presents is set aside, and people indulge in the national pastimes of eating, drinking, loving, and shopping. Even in the most remote sections of the country, after an hour's ride down rutted dirt roads, where horses far outnumber cars and families work their land and tend their chickens, the frame of a modest home will glow with Christmas lights at dusk and an evergreen will stand decorated in the living room.

In San José, the light show is spectacular, particularly in front of the children's hospital on Paseo Colón, where thousands upon thousands of tiny bulbs adorn the big tree overlooked by every window in the front of the hospital. Paseo Colón turns into Avenida Central, which is closed to cars from late afternoon into the evening, when roving pedestrians occupy the entire street. Many people ambling along have one of their hands entwined in someone else's hand, while the other hand manages something to eat. Confetti-throwing is another major activity. People shower each other in white flecks, so that by evening, as the street empties, you can almost believe that a miraculous white Christmas has arrived. "We love to imitate the United States so much," says one young sidewalk musician surveying the street, "that we even try to make snow."

Actually, San José has been visited by stranger showers than either snow or confetti. The awesome volcano Irazu, about twenty miles northeast of the capital as the ash flies, has a habit of erupting at least once a century. This being Costa Rica, even the volcanoes behave in a somewhat benign fashion: Irazu and the other active volcanoes in the country do not explode like Mount St. Helens, destroying everything in sight; nor do they spew molten lava like their Hawaiian cousins. They blow volcanic ash and dust over hundreds of square miles.

The last time this happened was 1963, at precisely the time John F. Kennedy visited San José to celebrate the Alliance for Progress, to give impetus to a Central American Common Market—and to try to take people's minds off the Cuban Bay of Pigs disaster. Volcanic ash was descending from the dark skies like a biblical plague, but that didn't stop a quarter million Costa Ricans from turning out on the streets of the capital to see the young president who actually seemed to care about the less privileged nations of the world (particularly when they offered a successful alternative to communism). "We will build a wall around Cuba," he told Costa Rica. "Not a wall of mortar or brick or barbed wire, but a wall of dedicated men determined to protect their own freedom and sovereignty." It was only a brief stop for Kennedy, one of the last he would make abroad. But his influence would linger, particularly in the mind of a young Costa Rican who was attending Boston University at the time of Kennedy's election: Oscar Arias.

Irazu's *ceniza* (volcanic ash) did more than linger; it dominated San José and much of the country for almost two years. Reports of how much ceniza actually fell vary from 3 million to 80 million tons, but even the smallest estimate is incomprehensibly large. Ceniza storms reached all the way to the Nicaraguan border, but were especially heavy on the Central Plateau around San José. Thousands of small farmers had to evacuate their land, coffee plants were killed, tens of thousands of head of cattle had to be moved or butchered prematurely, grain had to be washed before it could be fed to the livestock. In the city, people hoisted umbrellas at all times, women wore veils and scarves over their heads, dishes had to be rewashed moments before every meal, and urchins made steady money cleaning out gutters. To this day the top of Irazu looks like an eerie, gray moonscape on which only the heartiest of plants have managed to take root.

But here's another Costa Rican twist of fate: As bad as it was to have Irazu's insides all over the countryside, when the storm finally subsided it left behind what qualifies as the most productive soil in the world. The volcanic ash was absolutely loaded with life minerals, the essence of the planet. As soon as people could start planting again, by 1965, they saw fantastic harvests. Agriculture did more than resume, it redoubled—and all the United States relief aid that came pouring into the country during the worst of the ceniza certainly helped tide people over. Costa Rica's luck held yet again.

Now there is no soot to dim the gleam of San José plate glass by day or the shine of neon by night. And perhaps it

is the night more than the day that sets San José apart
from the rest of the country. By day you can see San José
as nothing more than an overgrown town. But at night it
has a spontaneous combustion common to big cities that
campesinos do not experience in the village, and it can be
both frightening and hypnotic.

Cruising through downtown, among heavy car traffic,
with lights everywhere, you can see plenty of movie the-
aters open for an early show. First-run U.S. films take a
little while to reach San José, so *Crimenes del Corazón*
(Crimes of the Heart) showed up six months or so after its
initial release, in English with Spanish subtitles. Richard
Chamberlain stars in *En Busca de la Ciudad Perdida* (In
Search of the Lost City), a movie you could search for in
the States and never find. Meanwhile, Sala Garbo is offering the classic version of *Anna Karenina,* while over at
Teatro Laurence Olivier, *La Muerte de un Burócrata,* the
satiric *Death of a Bureaucrat,* is advertised as *incon-
veniente niños,* not appropriate for kids. Of course, *La
Bamba* continues to draw them in.

The crowd drawn to Vicki Carr, performing on the outskirts of the city at La Cariari Hotel, is decidedly more
upscale. As women in heavy makeup and low-cut dresses
arrive escorted by men in carefully cut suits and Gucci
shoes, the scene is definitely about money. The couples
leave their BMWs or Mercedes out front (with or without
a driver). Tickets run around twenty-five dollars a head,
and if you want to drink, you have to buy full bottles of
liquor, which run from forty dollars to one hundred fifty
dollars.

Remember, this is not Atlantic City, this is Central
America. There has been a war in progress 150 miles to
the north, and a revolution taking shape 150 miles to the

south. Nevertheless the hall is packed, and if ever an example was needed to show that many Costa Ricans have money to burn, this is it. Carr's perfect Spanish (she lived in Puerto Rico) pleases the crowd, as does her broad, loud Las Vegas–style performance.

The casinos that dot the city are much smaller and more intimate than the Las Vegas version, but money still turns into chips, the chips get pushed and pulled just as fast, and the "free" liquor induces bravado just as effectively. Costa Rican casino rules are nationalized, and while the rest of the world plays blackjack, in Costa Rica they play *veinte y uno* (twenty-one). The distinction is that when you hit a blackjack (twenty-one with two cards), a fairly common event at the tables, the dealers do not reward you with a double jackpot the way they do everywhere else. Instead, if you catch triples, for example, triple sevens, you get five times your bet back. But triples happen only once in a blue moon, so the odds are against you. Yet the house makes up for that stinginess with a variety of subtle rules in the public's favor: You can double any bet, you can split any pair and play two hands, you can surrender any hand that looks like a sure loser and give up only half your stake. You don't get the easy blackjack money, but if you're smart and sharp and know what you're doing, the odds turn in your favor—exactly the way opportunity and success are seen in Costa Rican society.

At Key Largo, San José's most notorious bar, there is one sense of opportunity in the posh gambling room upstairs and another in the teeming bar below. The place is a century-old converted sea captain's house, in the middle of the city, which has been variously described as "loosely patterned on Bogart's [café in] *Casablanca*," "one of the world's great bars," and "a gloomy colonial mansion where one is apt to be set upon by aggressive tarts." The beautiful toucans that live in a cage beside the back-room restaurant don't seem to mind that the television sets constantly blare MTV off the satellite dish, interrupted only by a live band that plays most nights of the week. To call the women who line the bar "aggressive tarts" would not be right, although they certainly do make themselves available for a price, and when the police demand to see their health cards, they jump.

Even here, the sense of desperation is somewhat muted by the relative prosperity of the society. One woman will talk about how she is only one research paper away from her mechanical engineering degree but can't quite get it done, especially while her boyfriend is holed up in her apartment high on coke too much of the time, and she knows she has a problem coming to terms with all this but she and her analyst agree that now is not the right time to make a clean break. However, for many of her compatriots who have come to San José from rural Costa Rica without much money or education, the choice seems to come down to being a maid, a streetwalker, or a combination of both.

It's not a pretty picture. And there's much debate about why prostitution seems to be more common than ever in San José and what to do about it. Yet, without meaning to be heartless, without ignoring the personal tragedies, this is the kind of debate that could go on in the United States just as easily as Costa Rica. It is the debate about exploitation and capitalism reduced to the most physical expression. The desperation of absolutely no alternative, except starvation, does not override everything that could be said.

Only a few blocks from Key Largo, something much more heartening and less cynical is happening. In the back room of a small bar where the brick walls are painted white to make the place feel less cramped, a young crowd has gathered to hear the music of a local band named Canto America. It's a group that came together from associations around the University of Costa Rica, musicians scrounging for equipment and gigs. But despite all that, it's a tight group, solid and inspired. Two percussionists lay a beat with a bass player, backing three more musicians who make various combinations of two guitars, a flute, keyboards, and an old stringed instrument fashioned from a gourd.

The set makes people move, but the music is hard to characterize. It's not salsa, exactly, although it has salsa rhythms. It's not reggae, although the backbeat is heavy and the words are sung in Caribbean English at times. It's not calypso; it's much more complicated than old calypso, with melodic patterns that keep tumbling forward rather than coming to a clear end and then repeating. It's certainly not jazz, although at times the percussionists take extended breaks, and improvisation is definitely built into the form. It's something all its own, music that is not what people would call typically Costa Rican but that could emerge only in Costa Rica.

Manuel Monestel is the group's prime mover, the reason the music takes a unique shape. Dark, bearded, and well educated, Monestel can apply an intellectual's understanding to the emotions of playing good music. His influences vary greatly. On the one hand he can talk about the old folk music of Costa Rica's Central Valley, which celebrates "the peasants who founded the cities." The songs don't talk about social conflict as much as love and they romanticize the land. People were writing songs about campesinos fifty, one hundred, even one hundred and fifty years ago, singing lyrics like, "One day I'll have a piece of land, an ox cart, a beautiful woman; then I'll be like a king and envy no one." Or from Guanacaste there might be a cowboy song about how beautiful a man's horse is. Monestel can also ramble on about the Grateful Dead and want to hear more about the influence of the Talking Heads on contemporary rock music.

But most of all, Manuel's music is attempting a fusion of salsa, which is popular among the Spanish majority of Costa Rica, with calypso, reggae, and even rhumba, which are the sounds of Costa Rica's Atlantic Coast. He has searched out the older black men who still play the calypso forms, mostly disregarded by their own next generation, which prefers Bob Marley and the tougher, more electrified sound of Jamaican reggae. These men seem bemused that a Spanish man, a "pañamahn," as they say in the blend of Spanish and Caribbean patois known as Spanglish, takes an interest in their culture. But they sing him songs and show him calypso licks.

The music asks a lot of questions. Why is there a pocket of black Caribbeans in the middle of Central America? How did they get there, and why did they come? How do they fit into Costa Rican society, which is always referring to itself as homogenous, European? And if these two cultures have existed in Costa Rica for a long time, why is Manuel Monestel's attempt to fuse them so unusual, so new?

To search out the answers, you have to leave San José on a slow train, headed east.

CHAPTER FOUR

Train Travel, Time Travel

"One ticket, one way."

"*Sí, noventa.*"

Ninety colones, that's about $1.30 for a 102-mile, seven-hour trip from the Atlantic train station in San José to the Atlantic Ocean at the outskirts of Limón, from 3,000 feet above sea level to the shore, from the end of the twentieth century to the end of the nineteenth century.

The ornate old San José train station, symbol of the time when the train was the be-all and end-all of transportation, is now closed and dilapidated, awaiting historical restoration. Tickets are now sold from a hole in the wall on the other side of the narrow-gauge tracks. The diesel locomotive with a short string of passenger cars, ancient rolling stock with windows that actually open, stands ready to make the trip to Limón one more time.

"Sit ovah deere, mahn," an old black vendor tells me as he passes down the aisle, pointing to the right side. "See bettah." And then he walks on, sliding into Spanish, chanting, *"Maní maní maní maní!"* Peanuts.

It was 1890, after nineteen torturous years, that this railroad finally arrived in San José. It was the dream of General Tomás Guardia, who orchestrated a coup and came to power in 1870. Guardia was one of the Costa Rican leaders who defied categories, contributing to the foundation of democracy even as he contradicted its principles. After he seized power from Jesús Jiménez, the general silenced dissent and broke the power of the leading coffee families. At the same time he helped advance and fund public education, abolished capital punishment, and set up a national constitution. But most of all, he had a wild dream to build a railroad that would connect San José and Limón, to lay track "where the birds can barely fly," as people said at the time.

Not long after Guardia proclaimed himself president, he contacted Henry Meiggs, a builder from the United States who already had laid railroad track in Chile and Peru. Meiggs put the job in the hands of his nephew, Minor Cooper Keith, who turned out to be stubborn, lucky, shrewd, resilient, and charismatic enough to get the job done—even as men were dropping like flies around him.

"Refresco," another vendor sings. Refreshments for a long trip, which is about to begin. *Thunk*, the brake releases, and the train pulls out of the station.

One of the best things about trains anywhere is that

they slice through cities and countrysides on their thin rails; they don't have to wipe out six lanes worth of land to make room for enough asphalt to get from here to there. They become intimate with their surroundings. Within minutes of leaving the station the train is moving among the backyards and small coffee plots of San José. A young slender woman emerges from the back door of a small shack, two rooms with a corrugated tin roof on a postage-stamp yard, wearing bright high heels and a print dress, checking to see if the bleached laundry on the line is dry yet. And then a stand of 75-foot-high bamboo blocks the view.

Even as far as the track itself is concerned, this is a trip back in time, because Minor Keith and his men began their work at the seaport in Limón, within a stone's throw of where Columbus landed, facing west toward San José. Seven hundred men had left New Orleans and sailed across the Caribbean in 1870 to begin the labor. Maybe they thought that first stretch would be the easiest, because this is the flat alluvial plain before volcanic mountains rise up thousands of feet. But that wasn't taking into account the treachery of lowlands, of swamps and the diseases they carry. Within weeks, half the imported men had malaria and yellow fever. Six hundred of the seven hundred would die before long. Among the early ones to go was Minor Keith's older brother, Henry Meiggs Keith, named after the uncle who had gotten them both into this disastrous project.

Facing east, the San José suburbs pass out of sight, the rich green of coffee occupies more of the vista, single whitewashed homes sit on hilltops, but before long denser housing on tight side streets and then a bustling market announce the first big stop, Cartago, fourteen miles along the way. The train lurches to a halt, a few people jump on and off, young men and boys walk along the side of the cars selling bread, sausage, and ice cream. None of this deters the vendors inside (who are along for the whole ride). As the train moves into motion again, their calls continue. *"Manzana manzana manzana americana,"* chants one. Apples, American apples. *"Manzana manzana manzana, americana, manzana manzana . . ."* Suddenly he stops his call, puts down the tray that holds all the apples, looks out the window, and fervently crosses himself. Just as suddenly the tray is back on his hip, and the call picks up again.

Rising above the bustle of the market is a cross atop the arching roof of the basilica of Cartago. This is not a place the devout ignore. Indeed, hundreds of pilgrims from all parts of the country visit Cartago to pray at the church, coming any time of the year but especially on August 2. It is said that on that day in 1635, a young girl was walking in what was then a forest and saw a small statue of the Virgin perched on a rock. She took the beautiful thing home and stuck it in a box. The next day, as she took her walk, she saw another statuette in the very same place. She took that one too, but when she opened the box to add it to her collection, she found that the first image of the Virgin had vanished. Yet a third time, exactly the same thing happened, at which point she took her story to the village priest. The priest listened, went to the rock, saw the Virgin, and had exactly the same three-day experience as the girl. It was decided that a shrine must be built at the site of this rock, where a small stream also flowed.

In the centuries that followed, despite volcanic eruption and earthquake, the church at Cartago grew. The rock still sits in the basement of the church, and the stream still runs alongside. Thousands of people believe that the water of the stream has powers to cure injuries or handicaps and to help them survive surgery. Along the wall on the inside of the church are thousands of tiny trinkets symbolizing the parts of the body supplicants need healed. There are feet, fingers, eyes, arms, and legs, even hearts, stomachs, lungs, and livers. Most of them are silver and could be worn as little pins. They are faith incarnate; the apple seller crossing himself on the train seems more like a man hedging his bets.

Minor Keith could have used a few miraculous faith healings, but he didn't get any. They say a man was buried for every tie laid over the first twenty miles of track. That's an exaggeration, but not outrageously so. Before the project was done, four thousand people would die. Keith not only lost his older brother Henry but his younger brother Charles as well. Maybe Minor was a believer. Somehow, the plague did not touch him.

The real miracle Keith found, the only reason he was able to keep moving forward, was the importation of hundreds of Jamaican workers, many of whom had acquired an immunity to the swamp fevers that carried away other men. These black Jamaicans almost literally carried the railroad across the country on their backs. They stuck together, partly because they spoke a different language from the rest of the country and partly because they were considered low-life owing to their black skin. They set up their own churches, English and Protestant rather than Spanish and Roman Catholic. They read papers sent from Jamaica and listened to the faint English-language radio stations that wafted across the gulf. Even when the railroad was finished, many chose to live in towns along the

Atlantic, where they fished and hunted much as they had done in Jamaica, built wooden houses on stilts to cool themselves and keep animals out much as they had done in Jamaica, and, before long, worked the banana fields of United Fruit much as they had done in Jamaica.

Beyond Cartago, the climbing begins. The suggestion to sit on the right side of the train begins to make sense: The panoramas open out to that window, while on the other side the steep wall of the mountain is all there is to see. Behind small homes where barbed wire doubles as clothesline, the train's arrival brings families onto the porch: a diapered baby in Dad's arms, the next youngest sucking his thumb near Mother's skirts, the oldest girl waving. They stare as people everywhere stare at trains, listening to the whistle and the hypnotic *chug*, thinking about other places and strange travelers. Soon the land will become so rugged and remote that the few remaining houses will cluster around small settlements. The rest will be left for mountain coffee and wilderness.

By 1884, Minor Keith was out of the flatlands and into that wilderness, trying to work his way up the tortuous sides of volcanoes. But he was also out of money. The project had saddled Costa Rica with the scourge of an international debt, a malady that has lingered on and off ever since. The visionary who started it all, General Guardia, was dead. Guardia's brother-in-law, Próspero Fernández, was wrapping up his few years in power, preparing to turn the government over to his son-in-law, Bernardo Soto.

It was Soto who renegotiated with Keith and hit on one of those deals that made eminent sense at the time, like the Indians selling Manhattan and the French selling Louisiana: In return for building another fifty-two miles of track and funding the national debt, Keith was given a ninety-nine-year lease on the railroad right-of-way, plus ownership of eight hundred thousand acres along its corridor. He imported roots of a plant called the banana, planted them along the railroad, and kept his crew busy laying ties.

"Plátanos plátanos plátanos!" Bananas have replaced apples on the vendor's tray. Climbing along the volcano we see places so high, yet so warm, that evergreens and bananas can grow side by side. At Turialba the train is still closer to San José than Limón, even after hours of travel, but this is near the end of the slower ascent. Between brief stops at remote villages the wild countryside reasserts itself and the train's only hope of getting through is to slide along the shoulders of ravines cut by raging rivers. The sun shines on huge boulders exposed in the riverbeds. Above them a wire gleams: A pulley allows a box to travel over the river with messages and goods. The tracks also glitter as they turn onto a bridge over the gorge. The engineering feat of that bridge suddenly seems colossal. All heads are out the window. The mountain is an insurmountably huge green thing straight ahead. Then the train is suddenly engulfed in absolute blackness. People scream. It takes a few heart-in-mouth moments, but there is a light at the end of the tunnel and, then, the mountain is behind.

The countryside refused to be as benevolent to Keith as the government. He tried to skirt the northern slopes of the big volcanoes Irazu and Turialba, which would have been a more direct route into San José, but one river in particular would have none of it. Its name was Toro Amarillo, Yellow Bull, and not only was it wild and powerful, it was unpredictable and uncontrollable. A bridge would be built over the river, but Toro Amarillo would suddenly change course, washing out the railroad bed and leaving the bridge high and dry. Keith finally had to back up mile after hard-fought mile, resurvey, and take the railroad south of the volcanoes.

That route was difficult too. The mountains kept falling in on the track, killing people and destroying weeks of labor. As if conditions weren't bad enough, a variety of indigenous poisonous snakes, coupled with a cash flow problem that led to late payment of wages, kept the fear of mutiny fresh in Keith's mind. Yet neither snakes nor revolts could do what malaria and yellow fever could not. Keith survived—and so did his bananas.

On the eastern slope of the volcano, descending through Bonilla, Pascua, San Antonio, El Rubi, Las Lomas, Florida, and La Junta to Siquirres, four and a half hours from San José, the banana lowlands really begin and the extent of Minor Keith's agricultural achievements begins to become apparent. The tourist version of the train stops at Siquirres because a four-and-a-half-hour trip is enough, and the drama of the highlands is soon replaced by a swampy monotony. But this is where the railroad really has had an impact on the country for decades. Here the train picks up speed as daylight begins to fade and the poorest part of Costa Rica is exposed. Homes are all wood instead of concrete and stucco; many are without windows. At a town called Bataan, a Ferris wheel has arrived for a little carnival celebration. It is surrounded by a crowd of people.

Minor Keith helped whet the North American appetite for the banana, and by 1899 he had helped form United Fruit. Keith not only lived long enough to drive the railroad through to San José and see his bananas root, but before his death in 1929 United Fruit was employing as many as five thousand men in Costa Rica and shipping twenty thousand to thirty thousand bunches of bananas a day from the Limón seaport. There was a time when Costa Rica's national budget was smaller than United Fruit's operating expenses in the country.

There are other cultivated products of this tropical wetland, such as coconuts, cacao beans, and sugarcane. But the banana was king, at least while Minor Keith lived. Strangely enough, almost as soon as he died the Costa Rican bananas were struck by the deadly Panama disease, wiping out thousands of acres of crops and plunging the Atlantic Coast into deep depression. United Fruit pulled up its roots and moved all the way across the country to the Pacific Coast, where a flat swampy plain along the ocean mirrored the Atlantic. The high mountains stopped the Panama Disease, and new ports, company towns named Quepos and Golfito, sprang up to service the new banana plantations.

But the employees of United Fruit did not move with their jobs. The black Caribbean people around Limón were not allowed to live in communities past Siquirres. Nor were they allowed to vote. They *were* allowed to stay put and to struggle in poverty. Slowly, a new kind of banana, more disease-resistant, would return. But that would come only after a generation, after a good deal of violence and despair.

The train now speeds through the lowlands, past towns with names that reflect dual heritages, past Margarita and Boston, Toro and Buffalo, Liverpool and Miramar. The sky becomes black, except near the refinery on the outskirts of Limón where a supernaturally bright flame of wasted gas burns at the top of a stack, lighting even a stray low cloud. And then finally, anticlimactically, after seven hours and fifty-six stops, the train lurches to a halt. It is the end of the line—Limón.

From the buildings wedged together at trackside a few blocks from downtown comes the sound of Spanglish. Initial impressions reveal a naked light bulb beside the eerie blue of a television screen, a fire in a drum, dinner on the porch, an impassive stare at the train travelers. Limón is a quintessential port town, rough, hardnosed. Sailors from around the world slap ashore here, fresh off the decks of anything from a U.S. warship to a Liberian freighter. They're looking for action, which certainly can be found.

Along the main streets of downtown there is an impressive ratio of bars per square block. They can be full any night of the week depending on the schedules of the shipping lanes, which do not abide by nine-to-five, Monday through Friday. The custom seems to be to leave all empty beer bottles on the table in front of the drinkers, probably so there will be no fights about the tab at the end of the night. There also seems to be a custom to drink until foreheads fall on the only bit of formica tabletop not occupied by beer bottles. In one bar a scratchy guitar and the syncopated bass throb of reggae music fill the air; next door the flourish of Spanish guitars dominates.

Limón's park is not in the center of town, nor attended by an ornate church, as would be the case in a Spanish village. It reaches down to the seawall, where the English put a park, full of tall palm trees whose trunks are painted white. At night, the lights of the port line the shore, arching into the Caribbean, where breakwater and deep water combine to attract the big ships of commerce and tourism. While bananas still move off the pier, there are now many other things too, from shrimp to lumber. And rumors persist that cocaine from the south finds its way north through Limón, while guns from the north work their way into Central America at these same docks.

None of that seems to matter to the teenagers gathered on the seawall. They have the ocean in back of them, the park in front of them, and a big boom box alongside that blares music by Yellowman, a Jamaican albino reggae star. "Nobody move," he raps, "Nobody get hurt." The guys ignore the advice, showing off for the girls by pulling wheelies on their bicycles. They could easily pass for kids in a park along Jamaica's coast, at Port Antonio, for example, where United Fruit got its start. But they are Costa Rican born and raised, as Costa Rican as anyone on the Central Plateau. *"Vamos!"* shouts the teenager closest to the music. He hoists the box on his shoulder, and like the Pied Piper lures them all down the street.

The clack of billiard balls punctuates noisy conversation from a second-story pool hall, drifting down over an inordinate number of Chinese restaurants. In fact, as you get to know the city a bit, you realize that the Oriental community not only is strong but tends to dominate the retail business scene. Thrown into the same boats as the Jamaicans by the long arms of the British empire, "Chinese coolies," as they were wrongly called, also participated in building the railroad. It is one more way that Limón is like Jamaica: The children of these "coolies" became the shopkeepers and entrepreneurs of their villages, a progression apparent on the Caribbean island as well.

The teenagers have seen and heard all this a thousand times and pass by in step with the rhythms of Yellowman's reggae. None of them would dream of listening to the old calypso that their grandparents sang. Yet the calypsonians sang about what was happening on Costa Rica's Atlantic

Coast, not Jamaica's Atlantic Coast, and they saw themselves as the voice of culture. For example, there is the calypso about the "Chineemahn" who is passing by a calypsonian in a chance encounter. He is angry about nothing, or everything, and begins cursing the calypsonian's mother, calling down black people, but speaking only in Chinese. The calypso singer imitates sing-song Chinese in the song as he describes the scene. But the Chinaman is in for a shock—the calypso man knows exactly what he's saying!

"Don't keep cursing my people down," says the calypsonian, "or I'll turn your country into a toad."

The Chinaman realizes he has stumbled across an *obeah* man, a Jamaican term for a man with strong powers, almost comparable to a voodoo priest. He becomes fearful. But as the song ends, there is a twist, much like most calypsos twist: Instead of lording it over the Chinaman, the calypsonian suggests that they cooperate and share. The social allegory is clear.

Of course, cooperation was not a big part of United Fruit's schemes in Central America. As early as 1913, workers in the banana plantations were agitating for better conditions. They were not very successful, and their leaders were killed, but they set the stage for a strike in the 1930s that began to swing the balance of power away from United Fruit in Costa Rica. Before much longer, Costa Rican society once again was able to turn an exploitive situation into one of the more benign and beneficial relationships between a multinational corporation and a Central American government.

Costa Rican Communists deserve a lot of the credit for this evolution, although it was revolution they wanted. Manuel Mora, who started perhaps the first Communist party in Central America, came to Limón from San José in the 1930s and began organizing workers much like grass-roots Communists in the United States organized unions during the Great Depression. Demands covered everything from housing to medical care. There was a strike, violence, and hard bargaining. And there were results, both direct and indirect, from all the pressure: In 1935, the Costa Rican government and United Fruit agreed that 250,000 acres of its land should be distributed in fifty-acre plots to local growers. What's more, many of the demands of Mora's fledgling union were met. The foundation was laid for yet more reform over the next two decades, when United Fruit would pay some of the best wages in Central America to its Costa Rican workers, plus provide decent medical care, plus kick back a percentage of its locally grown profits into Costa Rican coffers, which reached 35 percent. It was a mutually beneficial relationship that other nations of the region would come to admire and emulate.

But by 1940 United Fruit had gone to the Pacific Coast, escaping disease, soil weakened from decades of banana crops, and militant workers. So the benefits passed by Limón to a large extent. What remained was the train, which as recently as 1970 was still the only reliable land route from the Atlantic Ocean to San José. And if Limón's population remains bitter at inhabiting the poorest part of the country, at being neglected and even discriminated against, they do not often express it.

"How doing, sweets?" a man asks in the morning light, hustling toward work.

"*Bien, usted?*" the woman he addressed answers, smiling. Good, and you?

"Not so good like you, yah know," he grins, winking.

She leaves him to do some shopping at the open market in the center of the city, and there is ample proof that even in Limón, where Costa Rican society is said to work least well, food is not a problem. Row upon row of fresh fish meets slab upon slab of bright red meat, while chickens hang near mounds of oranges. Bags of rice support bags of beans. There's enough money around to support the sale of trinkets and gum, cigarettes and toys.

The market might be dirtier and more crowded than markets in other cities of Costa Rica, but then again, if it were picked up bodily and dropped down in a comparable city of almost any other Central American nation, it would be a showpiece of variety and quality. Indeed, walking the streets of Limón by day, dodging cars and taxis, returning nods from men with dreadlocks sitting on benches, squeezing around knots of animated conversationalists who fill up a sidewalk, the sense is not one of poverty. There is something else at work in Limón, something that Costa Ricans by and large don't appreciate. It is not just the ethnic allure of Jamaican and Chinese mingling with Spanish, although that's part of it. It has more to do with a feeling of depth in the town, that what you see is only the latest of many incarnations, that Limón survives comings and goings, disease and depression, railroads and bananas, and maintains a certain essential character. More than any part of Costa Rica, Limón feels like a Gabriel García Márquez town, like Macondo in *One Hundred Years of Solitude,* rising and falling, circling back on itself, full of bittersweetness to those who understand its history. On the Central Plateau, around San José, Costa Ricans tend to miss that point: Many people in San José see no reason to go to Limón, and indeed many never have.

But if it needs to be hammered home that things in

Limón aren't half-bad, all it takes is a trip about three kilometers out of the center of town and up a few dirt roads to Pueblo Nuevo. Behind a barbed wire fence is Campamento Limón de Refugiatos, the refugee camp at Limón. There is an unfortunate similarity between the words *campamento* and *camposanto*, between *camp* and *cemetery*. The burials here have to do with hope.

The Limón camp consists of eleven barracks where as many as fifteen hundred refugees live at a time. Each barrack is not much bigger than a dormitory at a summer camp. There are more than one hundred people per barrack, separated only by whatever makeshift cardboard barriers they can erect. All of these people have come from Nicaragua, many of them from a town along the Caribbean coast known as Bluefields. The camp has long been a home to transplanted island people of black skin and English speech who crossed the Caribbean. Many Miskito Indians, who also live on the Atlantic side of Nicaragua, have found their way here as well. The common denominator is that everyone is escaping war, and escaping the Sandinistas.

Behind the barbed wire, seated on a block of wood outside barrack 8, sits Kenningston Garth Bonnas. He is a strong, quiet man, perhaps in his mid thirties, able-bodied, intelligent. It seems so incongruous to meet him in a refugee camp. He was a country man, a small farmer and fisherman on the Nicaraguan coast where he was born. There he lived a life that has been known and understood for centuries along the Caribbean—until the war came too close to home. He does not talk easily about the decision to leave, saying only that he felt the time had come to take a chance, to accept that there was less and less to lose by staying put. With his wife and daughter he climbed into a small boat in Bluefields, waited for the winds to be right, and three days later, plying the Caribbean, reached Costa Rica. It was not exactly the Promised Land; they were placed in the refugee camp at Limón.

That was a year and a half ago, and now Bonnas is alone. "My wife and daughter went back," he explains. "They couldn't stand the pressure. But I can't go back to the same situation. I have to move forward, somehow." Forward would mean working on the docks, perhaps, or on one of the cruise ships or merchant vessels that come and go from the port. But to do that you need working papers, and most of all you need a passport. Kenningston Bonnas cannot get that elusive document; he is a refugee who entered the country illegally. And so he sits.

Some people in the camp work, mostly in construction or as maids around Limón. They present their employment papers to the government people at the front desk, get stamped permission to exit, and earn enough to supplement the sugar, coffee, flour, rice, and beans that are provided to refugees for free. Simple economics says that it would be almost impossible for even the most hardworking person to save enough money this way to break out, to buy a little piece of land and begin farming or start a little business. And that, in part, is why some people have been in this camp for more than five years.

Limón is only one of a handful of refugee sites around Costa Rica. At various points during the last ten years, people have poured over the borders. Some say that 250,000 Nicaraguans came to Costa Rica in 1979 because of the war that ousted Somoza. Many returned, many did not, and many came later: In 1985, reputable sources were reporting five hundred "*nicos*" a day crossing the line. People have also come from El Salvador and Hon-

duras—left-wing, right-wing, and apolitical. The rich seek
asylum, the poor seek security and food. The influx has
put a real strain on Costa Rica, taxing national resources
and testing the Costa Rican self-image that this is a country of open arms. Everywhere there is talk about how
crime is on the rise, how violence has made its way into
everyday life as never before, and always people blame
the Nicaraguans, the aliens. "People give you a hard time
here because they know you're Nicaraguan," Bonnas says
simply, with a shrug.

But it is tough to blame too much on Kenningston Garth
Bonnas, as he sits behind barbed wire. He is clearly a
victim, not a criminal. As he walks through the camp, past
a communal kitchen where teenage boys who have no families cook their meals, past a public washing area where the
women clean clothes, past a makeshift church under a dirty
tent, past a mural on the side of a wall that shows a child-
ishly pretty picture of Bluefields (until you notice a trio of
helicopters descending) and that clashes so dramatically
with the stark camp around it. Bonnas repeats a little chant
he has taken up: "There's nothing like trying, nothing like
it. And if you don't try, nothing gets done."

At the far corner of the camp, where you'd least expect
it, is a symbol of trying: A boat, thirty-four feet long, dug
out of one huge tree that was felled at the edge of the camp,
nears completion. It is solid, well-crafted with good lines,
easily big enough for four men. It could fish the Caribbean,
no problem. Strong ribs are in place, most of them bolted,
but there is no paint on the wood and none of the finish
work has been done to protect the boat and get it into the
water. It seems that the man most responsible, one of Bonnas's friends, has not come up with the money to pay for
the hardware he's already used. If he doesn't soon, the boat

will be confiscated. Regardless, if he doesn't get the wood covered soon, the boat will begin to rot.

"So it stays," says Kenningston, and he says it in a way to make clear that this boat represents more than his hopes. It represents himself.

The *limoncense*, as they are called, understand what it is to be outcasts. Only in the 1950s, after nearly a century had passed, were the people of Limón granted full citizenship in Costa Rica—allowed to vote, to live wherever they choose, to be full participants in the national life. It was Don Pepe Figueres who recognized the inequality in the midst of his country and moved quickly to right a wrong during the months of his first government. In terms of civil rights, Costa Rica was a decade ahead of the United States.

This was a big moment for Limón Province, so of course the calypsonians created a celebratory calypso in Spanglish—with the ever-present tongue-in-cheek appearing at the end. The song is called "Figueres's Calypso," and the words go like this:

> *Por que Figueres nos ayudo*
> (Why did Figueres help us)
> *a la Provincia de Limón*
> (in the province of Limon)
> *Nos hizo ticos a muchos miles*
> (He made thousands of us ticos)
> *Nos dio la naturalización*
> (And gave us citizenship)
>
> Let's sing together
> Con Pepe sing
> (As Pepe sings)
> Viva Figueres!
> And vote for him.

Whatever the ulterior motive, it is certainly fitting that it would be Figueres, Costa Rica's political prime mover, who would cede rights to the limoncense. For a lesser man, this act alone would qualify for a major historical mention, but for Don Pepe it is only a footnote.

And leaving Limón, in search of the legacy of José Figueres Ferrer, you no longer have to take a slow train headed west toward San José. A brand new highway has finally cut through the mountains, so what has always taken seven hours by rail now takes little more than two hours by car. The quick access of the highway, even more than edicts from Figueres, is drawing Limón into full involvement with the rest of Costa Rica. Bets are that a generation from now, calypsonians and Spanglish will be things of the past.

INTERMEDIO UNO (INTERLUDE ONE)

Three Performances,
Three Nights

I didn't want to return directly to San José. I felt that something was eluding me, not a large mystery yet still something fundamental. I needed to prowl around, give whatever experiences the country wanted to offer their own time to reveal themselves.

The Pacific Ocean finally stopped me at a small, steamy town called Quepos. Maybe the flow of history had been pulling me here without my realizing it. Quepos is a company town, built by United Fruit in the 1930s when it escaped radical Limón, a place where workers could rest their bones and the company could ship its bananas. Upper management (often North American) lives in the cooler hills and handsome homes overlooking the ocean high above a cluster of a few run-down square blocks, which is downtown.

These days palm oil, not the banana, is king. Mile after mile of palm trees are planted in straight lines along the coast; when harvested the palm nut is heated and squeezed dry, the coarse husk burned as fuel to fire the factory's boilers. There was once all kinds of talk about how this oil could replace crude, lubricate engines and smooth the workings of the finest watches. But more realistically it has become the choice of potato chip makers and processed food manufacturers because it is sometimes even cheaper than soy. At Quepos the pungent scent of the oil seems to linger in the air.

Night had fallen fast the way it does near the equator; twilight does not linger. Billowing over the darkness I heard a voice amplified by a loudspeaker. "*Señores y señoritas,*" it boomed, "*bienvenidos a los toros en Quepos.*" Ladies and gentlemen, welcome to the bull-fights in Quepos.

At the edge of town I saw a strange stadium. It had been built out of raw wood, with poles pounded into the dirt in a large oval, two-by-fours crisscrossing and bracing here and there, one-by-threes tying into the two-by-fours, and planks of rough one-by-tens on top of everything. Yet somehow this arena had taken a classical shape, a miniature makeshift coliseum. Steps leading to seats angled back ten rows and could support several hundred people easily. Electric lights were set on tall poles. There even was a grandstand where an announcer overlooked the proceedings, accompanied by a band featuring six trumpets and a set of drums. The place was a building inspector's nightmare; in the United States, no one would go near it.

Down below, in the center of all this, the interior space was a bowl of pure mud. The announcer, talking excitedly, spoke the way radio announcers are supposed to speak before a big event, urgent and emphasizing every third word. The band broke into "Winchester Cathedral" and the crowd leaned forward on the planks, when suddenly the gate opened and out ran the bull, *el toro*.

He was a Brahma whose hump in the middle of his back was more impressive than the horns on his head, but he was a big fellow and when he stamped into the middle of the mud pit he commanded respect—even though he looked more confused than mad. *"El toro,"* the announcer shouted, *"y los torreros!"* The toreros, the bullfighters, awaited their challenge. There were three at once, and none would be mistaken for a Spanish matador. None wore shoes, let alone boots, so their feet were black with mud. Only two carried red capes to entice and enrage the bull, although, as they swayed slightly on their feet, their eyes probably were red enough to provoke the animal.

One of the three truly was brave. He got down on one knee in front of the bull, red shorts and yellow shirt sure to attract attention, and unfurled a cape that read *Romance Bar, Quepos* in gold letters stitched against a red background. The bull was somewhat aroused, and took a half-hearted run that was deftly parried. The crowd shouted appreciation, and then the bull began to lope around the ring, near enough to the stockade stands so that young boys could reach out and touch his back. Then he stopped again, confused once more, and looked about as if to say, "This afternoon you fed me, and now you want me to chase you around? This doesn't make sense." The matadors tried to entice him into another charge, running by and slapping his horns. Teenagers in the crowd, egged on by their friends, jumped in too and ran as close to the bull as they dared. When he moved so much as a hoof, most of them hightailed it for the wooden fence at the edge of the pit and jumped over to safety.

Before very long nothing would move the Brahma: he was played out, dazed. And so three cowboys galloped into the ring, their stallions prancing, ropes swirling in the air over their heads, and they took turns trying to lasso the beast. He gave them a steady target, his head and horns passive and waiting. The first two missed but the third made a perfect toss, tightened the noose, and led the bull back to the stall. The announcer, much excited, congratulated the cowboy, and the band broke into "Winchester Cathedral" again.

Next the announcer conducted a brief interview over the loudspeaker with a young man named Carlos who was about to ride a bucking bronco. Yes, he has done this before, said Carlos, but yes, it is always fearful. The announcer wished him well and the crowd hushed in anticipation—but somehow the bronco managed to get out of his stall before Carlos could mount him. The bronco bucked impressively, kicking up his heels and letting mud fly, but he was alone. Carlos, embarrassed, did not try again.

Then came the star bull of the night, "Diablo," as the announcer named him, *"un toro completo negro."* The gate opened and, sure enough, out charged a big black bull. He was of a different order from his predecessors. This bull had fire. He dropped his head, pawed the ground, looked for a place to vent his anger at being in this humiliating situation. He faced the bravest of the makeshift matadors, who again waved his Romance Bar cape, red shorts and exposed legs no doubt offering yet a more maddening incentive to charge. Diablo rushed— and that half-drunk barefoot matador executed a graceful sidestep, sweeping the cape over the horns in a thrilling gesture. The bull suddenly lost his fire. The audacious move robbed him of his indignation. He became content to lope around the pit while the teenagers scrambled out of his way. And when he tired of running, the cowboys came out and tried to lasso him. This time it took two horses to pull him in. The crowd applauded as Diablo vanished and the barefoot matador accepted his well-deserved congratulations. He didn't buy his own drinks at the Romance Bar that night.

This was quite a lighthearted rendition of what is usually a deadly serious, macho sport, I thought. Spaniards would probably ridicule and disdain such low parody, but I enjoyed this Costa Rican version of a bullfight. No swords, no daggers, no bull ears presented to the favorite lady. The drunken matadors, the teenagers in the crowd, even the bulls all seemed to be in on it together, to see the joke and not take themselves too seriously. I liked what I saw as a Costa Rican attitude.

Several nights later, still on the prowl, I found myself standing in the darkness again, hearing another voice booming through a loudspeaker into the night of another town. *"Señores y señoritas, bienvenidos a Liberia, La Ciudad Blanca."* Ladies and gentlemen, welcome to Liberia, the White City.

The capital of Guanacaste Province in the northwest, a jog off the Pan-American Highway less than forty miles from Nicaragua, Liberia is the big city of the wide-open cattle country of Costa Rica. It's a lot bigger than Quepos, with block after block of shops surrounded by suburban-style housing. And in the center of it all is a dramatic white church, with three modern triangular spires jutting upward and broad steps dropping down to the public park. In front of the church, with most of the town gathered in the park below, a major event was about to take place: The filming of a television show about Liberia and Guanacaste.

The television crew from San José had been working all day, setting up lights, checking equipment, running sound checks. "Sí, sí, sí," the sound man said over and over again. They had brought in materials such as bamboo, hay, and large plants to construct a set on the steps of the church that was meant to make Guanacaste look very primitive. That is the reputation of the province, and actually the land around Liberia does look a lot like the Australian outback, with long rolling hills covered by tall grasses, broken by the majestic spread of an occasional guanacaste tree. The modern abstract whitewash of the church wouldn't fit the image to be broadcast; neither would the tall transmitting tower rising above the buildings a block away.

On the stage, getting their last makeup touches, were the two people who would host the show. "Talent," they are called in the business, a handsome dark-haired mustachioed man matched by a beautiful dark-haired woman in a flowing dress. They were perfectly coiffed and looked great in the prepackaged way "talent" is supposed to look great. They greeted the crowd and explained that the show about to be taped would be broadcast as part of a cultural exchange with Mexico and Peru. It was meant to show other Latin people what Costa Rica is like, province by province. And so, at the beginning of the show, the hosts would say, *"Buenos días, Costa Rica!"* And the crowd should call back, *"Buenos días!"* Check.

The young teenagers running around the town square weren't paying much attention. They were too excited to be following such silly directions. That same afternoon a bunch of them had been hanging around the swimming pool at the local hotel, which doubles as a hangout spot for families on weekends. While their parents sat at the bar and ate some lunch, they had set up two garbage barrels, one at either end of the pool, and used them as baskets in a game of water basketball. "Michael Yordan!" the boys cried, trying to stuff a half-deflated soccer ball into the barrel. "Los Angeles Lakers!" And now, a big-time television show, right here in Liberia. *Fantástico*.

Cameras rolled, the theme song played, and the hosts were suddenly smiling and animated. *"Buenos días, México!"* shouted the woman. The crowd was confused; half called back, half did not. The producer held up his hand to stop taping. The man onstage, embarrassed, explained that first they would welcome Mexico and Peru, and then turn to Costa Rica. Later on, audiences from those two places would be inserted into the tape of the show. *"Disculpe me,"* he added. Forgive me for the confusion. *"Otra vez."* Once again.

The second time everyone got the idea, and the show was off and running. *"Buenos días"* everyone called at the right moment. Actually, it was a rather slick production. On the one hand were live acts from the area around Liberia, singers and musicians, young and old. They were dressed in traditional clothes: white cotton shirts with colorful printing and stitchery, broad cowboy hats of leather or straw. And there were pre-produced video pieces that had been shot and edited earlier showing interesting scenes around Liberia, or architecture, or unusual crafts. Between live acts, the hosts introduced the video segments, which bought time to rearrange the stage and move people on and off. To keep the crowd from getting restless, a large screen had been erected that played the taped segments as they would appear in the show and transmitted what the cameraman on stage was shooting during the performances.

As for the subject matter, well, that's an interesting aspect. Before long it became clear that this was not the most controversial, topical television the world has seen. Rather, it was meant to be cultural, maybe even mythical, talking about Liberia and Guanacaste in romantic terms. A young girl sang her love of the White City and the open plains around it. A storyteller wove a tale of the beauty of the town and land, the hardworking cowboys who ride the range, the need for sun and rain in good measure. A sculptor duplicated a handsome old building with a narrow porch overlooking the street.

It was a sweet, gentle picture, although it ignored most of what had been happening around Liberia of late. It was as if a show about Iowa romanticized the family farm but forgot to mention that it was in danger of disappearing. Even in the centuries before Guanacaste broke from Nicaragua and became a part of Costa Rica in the early 1800s, it had been a frontier and a place of opportunity, of ranches, cattle, hard work, and dreams coming true. Now the ranches are being consolidated into megatracts for agribusiness, and it is common for North American investors to own many thousands of acres. Throughout the country, people recognize that a profound thing is happening, a fundamental shift from the inspiring ideal of the proud, independent rancher roaming his range on horseback. And because Costa Rica is much like the United States, where free enterprise and private property rights are sacred, there doesn't seem to be a way to avoid this consolidation, this not-so-gradual pooling of land and resources into a few hands. If you have the money, you can own it, and if you own it, you can do pretty much as you please.

But the crowd that night was far from judgmental and political. It was festive, relaxed, familial. Mingling among this group of Costa Ricans I was truly touched to see how much plain and simple affection was expressed. There was nothing theatrical about it, or vicarious, or overblown. A chubby baby in her mother's arms got a big kiss on the cheek, then her father took her and gave her another before holding her over his head so she could see the singers onstage. Grandparents called out to the children scampering around, stopping them from their wild game of tag, straightening out their clothes and slicking down their hair, insisting that they stand still while they were hugged by a couple of relatives, given a few pieces of candy, told not to hurt themselves, and sent on their way. Young couples walked hand in hand, arm in arm, not needing wedding bands before they could show their feelings. One couple stole a kiss in the shadows behind an old tree—not that they were so hidden that a pint-sized prankster couldn't run by and pinch his older brother in the ass at just the wrong moment. A young married couple, clearly cleaned up and dressed for the evening, watched the stage intently. The wife's hand was on her husband's shoulder so she could stand on tiptoe without losing her balance. An older couple sat on a bench, at ease, more interested in friends passing by than in the entertainment. They had the right idea; the crowd was the real show.

An hour later, the "talent" was on their way back to San José. The television lights had been turned off, and so the thousands of moths that had been bent on destroying themselves in the heat of the glare could settle down and live another night. At the edge of town a lively crowd gathered to drink and talk in an open-air bar, hooting a welcome as a strolling band appeared with gleaming trumpets and flamenco guitars flourishing. At the intersection of the Pan-American Highway was the wayside restaurant El Bromadero, and everyone who entered walked past a statue cast from cement of a *campesino*, a cowboy with hat, lasso, and riding pants, carrying a high-horned saddle. He seemed to be watching the highway, more vigilant than welcoming, looking into the night at the latest asphalt version of an ancient road.

The concrete cowboy didn't know it, but only a few miles north he had a companion who was also watching the road. At a Rural Guard checkpoint, a man clad in U.S.-issue army fatigues searched the cars that passed his way.

This was not customs, this was a roadside stop miles before the border. The army man was polite: he didn't rip things apart, but he looked. After all, Nicaragua is not very far north of Liberia, and life on the other side is not the same as life on this side. Checkpoints and searches reveal the fear and uncertainty about what is happening around that border, and what could happen.

These are worries Liberians by and large push to the back of their minds. Why harp on it, they imply, when there is so much good at hand? In a small, isolated way, it is like learning to live with the threat of nuclear war. It is a part of Guanacaste Province, even if the television show didn't mention such things.

The next day I spiraled back toward San José, drawn to the center once more by cultural gravity. My timing was auspicious because that very evening another performance was unfolding, a real San José event. *Señores y señoritas, bienvenidos al Country Club Costa Rica*. Ladies and Gentlemen, welcome to the Costa Rica Country Club.

Brilliant lights above center court were all ablaze, and the grounds were crawling with spectators. The annual Costa Rican tennis tournament, which attracts many of the world's best players eighteen years and younger, had begun. This is a prestigious tournament to win and a prestigious tournament to host.

The Costa Rica Country Club was built by and for the modern coffee oligarchy, much as the National Theater was built by the coffee barons in the last century. The club's main building is an extraordinary blend of modern architecture and handsome indigenous dark woods, replete with ornate hand carving. Long, open verandas with cool, airy spaces counterpoint a formal interior room. Money was no object, and style is the message.

On the court, Carlos Muñoz, Costa Rica's only hope, was struggling to follow in the baseline footsteps of his father (one of Costa Rica's best). Carlos didn't look fully prepared for his sortie into the national spotlight. Before he knew it he had lost five straight games. "Carlitos!" cried an affectionate woman's voice in the crowd, using his nickname to urge him on. Carlos struggled back before dropping the first set, 6-2, then had a chance to go up 4-3 in the second but missed a crucial break point, lost the game, and then let the match slip through his grasp. On match point he drifted back to the service line for a short lob, set up for an overhead, and drove the ball into the net, falling on his back in the process. With a tico sense of drama he slowly picked himself up, dusted himself off, and bounced to the net to congratulate his opponent.

Everyone clapped, a little sad to see the local guy lose. But no one really expected him to get past the second round (if the first). The national pride had barely been scratched, let alone wounded.

Actually, for the roving bands of teenagers who had come to the club, this was strictly a social event where the point was to see and be seen. Teenage girls moved together, admiring the foreign players, who admired them right back. It was remarkable how many of these girls wore braces, something of an adolescent Costa Rican status symbol. Not far away, the silver in their mouths would make eyes go wide with envy. Not far away, the mere possession of teeth is a status symbol. But here at the country club, an oasis within the oasis that is Costa Rica, wealth allows the discussion to move to teenage crises on the order of who did and did not have tickets for the big outdoor rock concert by the Argentinian group arriving that weekend.

The match over, the crowd began to disperse. The fast-food stands made their last sales, and traffic filled the street in front of the club. The people who were leaving have the fortune not only to be Costa Rican, but to be among the upper class of Costa Rica. What's more, their wealth is not held against them. It does not make them kidnapping targets or likely candidates for Marxist expropriation. It does not inspire anger and class hatred, but perhaps some natural envy and even national pride.

All this would be even more true if it were possible to

be black, Jewish, or of Asian heritage and expect to be welcomed as a full member of the Costa Rica Country Club.

I found myself wondering what Jośe Figueres would think of all this, echoing a question that no doubt has been asked many thousands of times in Costa Rica over the last forty years. Most likely he'd enjoy the pageantry, I thought, and disdain the racism. But then again, Costa Rica's political prime mover, Oscar Arias's political god-father, has always been a difficult man to understand, let alone predict.

CHAPTER FIVE

The Revelation of José Figueres

As the sun sets on José Figueres's life and times, the shadow he casts keeps getting longer and longer. The chaff of controversy and contradictions that filled up forty years of political life is sifting away, leaving his twin accomplishments exposed: abolishing an army and solidifying a democracy.

That's what the history books will say, and in a general sense they'll be right. But what makes Don Pepe so fascinating, so outrageously Costa Rican, is the stuff of his life as much as his profound legacy. Vanity and vision, ego and egalitarianism, pride and principle, corruption and courage all meld together into a national personality. And so in this case, separating the wheat from the chaff is like taking the soul from the body; essence, yes, but without a lot of the human interest.

His father was a physician who arrived in the small town of San Ramón from Barcelona, Spain, with a pregnant wife and a desire to practice physical therapy. José was born September 25, 1906, making him Costa Rican by birth, Spanish by conception.

More specifically, as Figueres himself has said, he is Catalán by conception, referring to a particular ethnic group of Spain. It is a notorious stereotype among Costa Ricans, this Catalán personality. "He's Catalán," someone will say, rolling her eyes, letting that explain everything. The connotation, for good or ill, covers the following traits: stubborn, hardworking, single-minded, inflexible, proud, unyielding, opinionated, self-centered, self-righteous, principled, demanding, obstinate, and willful.

The Catalán blood runs hot in José Figueres. From the start he had headstrong ideas about what he should do and what he wanted to learn. His father wanted him to be a doctor, but he became interested in engineering. His father sent him to a strict, learn-by-rote school in San José, which he rebelled against. While still a teenager, Figueres decided to attend the Massachusetts Institute of Technology in Boston. This in itself was not a radical idea in Costa Rican society; many of the wealthier families sent their children abroad to be educated. But, of course, Don Pepe had to do things his own way. Within a few months, he had dropped out of MIT. His next four years in the United States would represent a self-education rather than an institutional education, and he would support himself rather than count on paychecks from his father.

In creating his own classroom and university, Figueres set up shop at the Boston Public Library. It became his alma mater, he would say. And his major had nothing to do with engineering or electricity, but rather the social sciences. The more Figueres read, the more he became absorbed in what today we might refer to as romantic socialism. Charles Fourier, for example, was a major influence. Fourier was a French philosopher who watched hard industrialism march across Europe in the nineteenth century and concluded that small, communal, independent communities were the way out of inhuman exploitation. In the 1840s, Brook Farm, only a few miles from Boston's library, had tried to carry out this utopian vision. Figueres, coming from a place where wholesale industrialization had not yet stamped its mold on society, where small independent communities were more than the stuff of dreams, envisioned another way.

That vision certainly involved the philosophies of communism and socialism, but the ideal Figueres pursued in the Boston library was far from the ideal Karl Marx pursued in the archives of the British Museum. Figueres's vision appealed to a noble human spirit, to romance and utopia. Rather than a coldly calculated analysis of capital as the prime mover of society and revolution by the proletariat as a means of wresting control of industry from exploiters, he saw a capacity for social justice within the framework of free enterprise, totally accepting the American dream of equal opportunity for all and toying with how community structures and government intervention could actually make that dream a reality. Living in Boston and then New York City during the 1920s, catching the spirit of everything from big-city American hustle to New England town-meeting populism, Figueres was not being indoctrinated into the evils of capitalism. Nonetheless, at various points in his career, people would label him a

Communist, meaning to smear him both at home and in the United States. This was a misreading of his intentions and allegiances. One of Figueres's closest confidants, Enrique Carreras, explained: "He was made a Socialist in Boston, not Moscow or Havana. Never has the United States had a more important influence on a Latin American political figure."

Don Pepe returned to Costa Rica just before the stock market crashed and sent the world into the Great Depression. His four years overseas were finished but he had no diploma. Instead he had a voracious appetite for books as well as work, and he combined the two in creating an extraordinary farm south of San José called La Lucha Sin Fin (The Endless Struggle), or more simply La Lucha (The Struggle).

In many ways, La Lucha was Figueres's attempt to turn Fourier's utopia into reality, and in many ways it succeeded a lot better than Brook Farm. La Lucha's main income came from hemp grown and processed in the farm's rope mill, which could be traded for machetes and shovels or sold for cash. Slowly, using his engineering skills and inventive mind, Don Pepe began harnessing hydropower from the rugged mountain rivers and expanding operations by manufacturing coffee bags as well as rope. Catalán stubbornness paid off during the lean years of the 1930s, rewarding Figueres with prosperity and acclaim by 1940.

What was even more extraordinary about this boondocks operation, located only thirty-five miles from San José but reachable only after many hours on horseback, was the social structure that grew alongside the hemp. Don Pepe established excellent schools for the people who worked at La Lucha and even set up a tutoring program. As the factory was using water-generated power, Don Pepe brought electricity to the twenty-five houses on the farm (before even San José was fully electrified), which meant that in the evening people had the light and time to practice their newly acquired reading skills. Figueres recognized that as people become more educated, their aspirations change, which could threaten the stability of the community. So the educational system continued to improve, turning out dozens of technicians, welders, and electricians, some of whom fanned out around the country and some of whom remained. In 1970, when the management of La Lucha decided it was time to introduce condoms into the community (despite a threat of Roman Catholic excommunication), the farm became religiously controversial. But it still survives, if sometimes barely. Some members of its six hundred families are third- and fourth-generation descendents of the founders.

While most people acknowledge the success of La Lucha, different people define that success differently. Some say that Figueres translated dreams into reality, proving that he was a pragmatic visionary with a deep commitment to the common good. Sweeping to the other end are those who see in La Lucha not much more than paternalism, a benovolent dictatorship that offers no real example to the rest of the country. The interpretations of Don Pepe's political actions vary just as wildly.

Yet in the years leading up to 1942, Don Pepe was not a political man. Because Costa Rican society is so small, he certainly knew the political and social leaders of the time, but he was occupied with La Lucha's development on the one hand and his extraordinary book collection on the other. The two hands would join: H. G. Wells's *Outlines of History*, advocating an armyless society, had obvious influence. After reading John Steinbeck's *The Grapes of Wrath*, Figueres embarked on a reforestation program, planting trees at La Lucha and even publishing a pamphlet in later years that explained that the lines of the trees should relate to the line the sun travels across the sky on the longest day of the year in order to assure the best growth. He began this planting fifty years ago, when Costa Rican timber seemed endless. Contemporaries thought him crazy, but severe deforestation problems today have proven him prophetic.

The political moment of no return for Figueres was the first week of July 1942, when he was nearly thirty-six years old. The world was in the midst of war, which reached into Costa Rica on the night of July 2, when a German submarine torpedoed a United Fruit ship loading cargo at Limón. The boat sank, the men on board were killed, and the incident became a national outrage. By July 4, parades that had been planned to celebrate Independence Day in the United States turned into ugly riots. Rampaging crowds destroyed property and looted businesses, ostensibly punishing Costa Ricans believed to have ties or sympathies with Nazi Germany. As always, that kind of justice really is no justice at all. Many innocent people were hurt physically and financially.

Figueres was particularly outraged by two things: First, the government in power, in his opinion, had been lax in enforcing wartime security measures that would have prevented the bombing at Limón. And second, far from protecting Costa Rican citizens from mob violence, the government seemed not only to have condoned it, but perhaps even to have encouraged it. Figueres could not tolerate this, and the personal object of his wrath was the President of Costa Rica, Rafael Angel Calderón Guardia.

THE REVELATION OF JOSÉ FIGUERES

Were it not for Figueres, Calderón would have been the seminal figure of Costa Rican politics in this half of the century. Instead, Calderón has been the foil, the long-standing opposition, to Figueres's plans. Charismatic and brilliant, Calderón had followed in *his* father's footsteps and become a doctor (satisfying his father as Figueres would not), establishing a successful practice in San José before entering politics. He was elected president in 1940 and set about winning over poor and working-class people with an ambitious reform program.

Calderón's platform was built on the teaching he had received in Europe, particularly in the left wing of the Catholic church, which was advocating strong measures to help the poor. But that didn't stop Calderón from aligning himself with the Communist party, led by Manuel Mora, which had strength in Limón because of the battles against United Fruit as well as a base in the poorest parts of San José. Calderón's social programs sound tame and familiar by today's standards: Social Security, minimum wage, eight-hour work days, child labor laws. But they were radical for the time and place and alienated the upper class.

More disturbing, these liberal ideas were not linked with a strong belief in electoral politics and due process; not only did Calderón seem willing to manipulate election results to suit his ends, but his government was confiscating property from people of German and Italian descent and reportedly giving the wealth to friends and supporters. Many people loved Calderón for what they saw as his compassion, his championship of the downtrodden. But this lack of respect of the voting process and private rights haunts Calderón's legacy. After all, how many dictators began in much the same way, charismatic populists who said that the ends justified the means? Calderón's means, as we will see, justified a revolution.

But in that first week of July 1942, the immediate question was whether anyone would publicly hold the government accountable for the lawlessness and destruction that had taken place. Figueres, the willful, stiff-necked Catalán, decided he was the one to do it. A friend's family owned and ran a radio station with a signal that reached across the capital. Figueres would use it to make his declaration.

Everyone, particularly Don Pepe, understood the risk involved. Civil liberties were not guaranteed; speaking out against the government in such a direct way was certain to provoke a response. But Figueres was determined, and on July 8 he took to the airways, ostensibly speaking for a new group of middle-class, university-based intellectuals known as Acción Democrática (Democratic Action) that had coalesced in the past two years. He attacked Calderón's government, accusing it of an inability to govern that had more to do with incompetence than corruption. Figueres was highly ironic, saying, "The police are now patrolling the streets in order to prevent last Saturday's riot, and the government is installing guns on La Uvita Island to prevent the sinking of the *San Pablo* [the United Fruit ship in Limón]."

It was shockingly direct criticism for Costa Rica, but before Figueres could really get going, police broke through the door of the station and dragged him away from the microphone. The scuffle was broadcast across the country. A government minister later referred to Figueres as "a poor devil" and "an unknown," but it was Don Pepe who had the last word as they hauled him off: "The police order me to stop. I won't be able to say what I think should be done, but I can sum it up in a few words: What the government ought to do is get out!"[3]

Overnight, Figueres became a national hero. He was sitting in a prison cell, but his notoriety could not be contained so easily. Calderón's adversaries used the moment to highlight their grievances, while everyone from university students to politicians to workers on La Lucha called for Don Pepe's release. Calderón, however, was adamant: He wanted the man out of the country, and given extraordinary wartime powers, the president could expel a citizen at his discretion. The choice left to Figueres was either to become an exile of his own will (meaning he could return of his own will) or be exiled by the government (meaning he might not be allowed to return). It was a matter of the lesser of two evils, although it couldn't have been an entirely unexpected predicament. On July 11, 1942, Figueres left Costa Rica for Mexico.

Exile lasted twenty-two months, and maybe the most interesting aspect of it for Costa Rican history was that Figueres was put in touch with a variety of expatriate thinkers and radicals from across Latin America. He began political writings, keeping informed of the doings in Costa Rica and relating his country to the politics of the rest of Central America. It was in Mexico, during these two years, that the Caribbean Legion, as it came to be known, germinated. The legion's avowed purpose was to oppose dictators throughout the area, and although it was composed more of thinkers than fighters, both groups were represented. Figueres declared that Calderón in Costa Rica was on the same road as the rest of the tyrants, only not so far along. Whether others believed him was not as important as the fact that Figueres was connected to a quasi-revolutionary international underground. When the time came, he would have access to weapons and a small cadre of fighters to help him wage a civil war. The help would prove crucial.

Figueres was still in Mexico during the Costa Rican presidential campaign that ended in February 1944 in a bitter election. Widespread violence, wholesale fraud, shootings and lootings marked the voting. Ballot boxes were stuffed and stolen, the voting process raped. By law, Calderón could not be reelected himself, but he did the next best thing, assuring that a man named Teodoro Picado was inaugurated. Picado may have been well-intentioned, but the word *puppet* has often been attached to his name. The government's credibility was withering away.

In the face of this weakness, Figueres returned in May of 1944. He was welcomed as a prodigal son during a festive parade through San José and made his way back to La Lucha, greeting thousands of friends and supporters along the way. But he could not return to his former isolation. His apolitical days were over. He moved into the thick of opposition politics, but he refused to be a candidate in the next election. Figueres had concluded that the electoral process was too corrupt. He felt a revolution was justified, but the rest of the country was not moving quite so fast. It would need one more outrage to push people over the edge, and when that outrage occurred, in 1948, they found Don Pepe there and waiting.

The 1948 election was the last straw, but throughout 1947 events undermined the administration. Calderón was allowed to run again because Picado was the sitting president, so he took to the hustings. His major opposition was Otilio Ulate, a newspaper editor more in line with the conservative and wealthier Costa Ricans. Ulate opposed Social Security, for example, as well as some of the laws that protected labor unions. Figueres, who did not agree with much of what Ulate had to say, felt that at least he wasn't a Calderón, so they presented a common front. Figueres believed Ulate at least respected the electoral process. This last point had become so important to so many Costa Ricans that a general strike called by Ulate and Figueres (among others) to force the government to accept the authority of an impartial election tribunal had enough strength to paralyze the country for nearly two weeks. *Huelga de Brazos Caídos*, it was called. Strike of the Fallen Arms, referring to people injured by government troops. In trying to get banks and shops reopened, the government turned to violence again, permitting the activities of roving bands of men shipped into San José from Limón by the Communists. They were from the political group Popular Vanguard, know as *mariachis*, and the government looked the other way while they looted stores and stole food. Such tactics alienated yet more of the populace, and when hundreds of women marched on the Presidential House demanding fair elections, the government finally caved in and agreed to respectable ground rules. Tempers cooled momentarily.

The election was set for February 8, 1948; the news was bad from the start. Amid charges and countercharges of fraud and intimidation, the results gave victory to Ulate. As the election tribunal was trying to figure out how to certify the honesty of the vote, a large number of ballots burned in a suspicious fire. Calderón's backers claimed that they had been cheated by allies of Ulate and Figueres, yet certainly their own hands were dirty. On March 1, Congress (with strong influence from Calderón's deputies) voted to annul the election of Ulate. Ulate and his supporters had been meeting not far away in San José when the house was surrounded, one respected political leader shot to death, and Ulate briefly arrested. Figueres was not there; he was already in the mountains near La Lucha, planning strategy for a civil war he had been insisting was inevitable.

The fighting started March 11, and it would continue for a biblical forty days and nights. Figueres was no military strategist, but his practical mind and personal bravery served him well. His first step was to take control of a remote airfield called San Isidro, a maneuver his troops managed with such success that they also seized three airplanes, workhorse DC-3s. The "air force" was put to use immediately, flying to Guatemala, where a cache of small arms was waiting, gathered and paid for by Figueres's contacts from the Mexico years. A handful of revolutionary fighters also jumped aboard. The weapons, in particular, would prove crucial.

In the first few weeks of fighting, Figueres and his men retreated into the mountains, unable to keep La Lucha from being occupied and destroyed, unable to do much head-to-head fighting with the army. But by early April, the tide of the war had turned. The government had split mainly between Calderón and the Communists, who were worrying about each other as much as they were worrying about Figueres. The confusion gave the rebels room to move. By April 10, Figueres launched a daring plan to airlift men into Limón while at the same time attacking Cartago. Somehow, with luck playing a big part, both moves succeeded. Limón fell easily, but the Cartago area, near San José, saw some of the bloodiest fighting of the short war.

By April 15, when Figueres clearly was in control and

the government was talking surrender, two thousand people had died in the various skirmishes. It is a small number by United States standards, but represents one in every three hundred Costa Ricans at the time; everyone seemed to know someone, neighbor or relative, who had fallen.

And just when it seemed as though it was over, Nicaraguan forces launched an invasion from the north, reaching as far as Quesada by April 17. Somoza in Nicaragua had backed Calderón in the civil war, and it was with Calderón's tacit blessing and encouragement that the Nicaraguans descended. There were rumors that Calderón and Picado would move their operations to Liberia, allowing the Nicaraguans to rout the last Communist strongholds in San José and then wipe out Figueres. But international opinion, in particular strong United States opposition, stopped Calderón and the Nicaraguans from finishing what they had started. The force that made them retreat was more diplomatic than military.

Strengthened, Figueres negotiated cease-fires and made it clear that he was going to take over the government at least for a short while. All his altruistic talk about upholding the elections was fine and dandy, and Ulate would get his rightful presidential seat. But while Figueres was fighting in the mountains, Ulate had been sitting in his apartment in San José, talking about compromise. Besides, this revolution, in Figueres's mind, was about many more things than election fraud. He was the real victor, and the spoils would be eighteen months at the head of a junta, with the power to reshape Costa Rican society. On April 28, Don Pepe led a triumphant parade through San José. On May 8, 1948, his junta was established.

People really didn't know what to expect from the man, or rather, many people had the wrong expectations. After all, he had been called everything from a Communist to a Socialist to a Nazi. His revolution had been backed by some of the wealthiest, most conservative Costa Ricans, who expected him to repeal the progressive social legislation of Calderón. He had been saved by the United States, yet the shadowy Caribbean Legion had lent arms and support on the fundamental condition that this was only the first of the sweep of revolutions that would remake Central America (and oust many U.S.-backed regimes).

As it turned out, just about the closest political analogy to Don Pepe's eighteen months in power is the beginning of Franklin Roosevelt's New Deal, when so much fundamental and radical legislation blitzed through a U.S. Congress overwhelmed by the size of Roosevelt's victory and the depth of the Depression. The analogy does not leap out of thin air; Figueres admired, even idolized, FDR and studied his administration closely. Yet he was not a mimic. Rather, he applied FDR's broad-minded approach to Costa Rican needs.

In short order, the Social Security system was bolstered and institutionalized to make sure it would not be ignored. Full voting rights for women were enacted. Minimum wage, low-cost health care, child support—all were realized beyond lip service. Even more shocking, every bank in the country was nationalized; the flow of money, said Figueres, should be in the public's control like the flow of water and mail. A 10 percent tax surcharge was levied, but only on the wealthiest Costa Ricans—a crude form of graduated income tax. An independent Supreme Tribunal was established with sole authority to run elections. Another tribunal dispersed compensation for all those who had been financially damaged by the war. When it turned out that Don Pepe and his friends seemed to benefit most from the dispersements, the junta was caught in its biggest and most damaging scandal. Public education was bolstered with more funding and public commitment. The Communist party was outlawed. National efforts to bring electricity to remote areas (much like the Tennessee Valley Authority) were pushed.

It was a hectic time, complete with another mini-invasion from Nicaragua, where Calderón and Picado had fled into exile, not to mention a brief coup attempt from within the junta. But Figueres, as was his nature, hung tough. He was reshaping Costa Rican government and society with his bizarre blend of guts and bourgeois values. "We are a government of the middle class," he would say again and again. He meant it, too, and he meant Costa Rica to be a nation of the middle class. This would make his brand of revolution much less romantic than Castro's was destined to be, but just as profound and in some ways more successful.

If there was one group inside Costa Rica that felt betrayed by it all, it was the oligarchy. "In order to finance the weapons for the revolution," Figueres would say years later, "I had to keep myself back from expressing all my thoughts to them." And then, in a classic Don Pepeism, he would add, "It wasn't that I lied to them, but I didn't tell them everything."

Ulate, the rightfully elected president waiting in the wings, represented their best hope. But even he was not going to go back on the promise of the revolution. In fact, as the months rolled along, people were beginning to wonder whether Ulate would ever really move into the

Presidential House. Figueres was solidly entrenched, and he seemed to have made a transition very few revolutionaries can handle: He was nearly as adept in the bureaucracy as he was on the battlefield. The middle-class manager side of his personality allowed him to make good government after the willful, charismatic side of his personality had fought to topple bad government. Such different facets rarely converge in one person. Close advisers to Figueres suggested that, at the least, he should proclaim that the 1948 elections were so tainted as to be null and void. Call new elections, they urged, and you're sure to win, which would give us four more years to carry out the objectives of the revolution.

Figueres would tell friends years later that he was sorely enticed by such arguments. "It was a great temptation," he would say, as though the power of government were like the apple in the Garden of Eden. But it was in this moment that his greatness emerged because he was able to put aside personal ambition for national ambition and big enough to see the difference between the two. When Figueres named his first stay in power "The Founding Junta of the Second Republic," he wasn't going off on some Napoleonic ego trip. He truly wanted to establish a new republic, and respect of the electoral process was an absolute cornerstone of the society he had in mind. He would turn the government over to Ulate and in so doing legitimize his dreams and actions. In that moment he became more than a man of the moment, a man of action. He became a statesman. And in 1953, when he could run for office without a hint of impropriety, he would win a commanding 65 percent of the vote.

But before all that could happen, Figueres had to take

care of one more piece of business while the junta was still in control: He had to get rid of the army.

It was the ultimate expression of Figueres's personality and genius. At first glance the notion was hopelessly romantic and dramatic, an action more suitable for Don Quixote than Don Pepe. But examined as public policy, the decision began to take a pragmatic life of its own. Figueres's heart and head provided the arguments: No army meant no antidemocratic power base for coups and violence. No army meant public money could go toward education, medical care, and housing, rather than weapons, uniforms, and barracks. No army suddenly elevated Costa Rica's moral position to a dizzy height: If anyone tried to invade, there was no conceivable way they could argue that they were provoked. He would place his trust in international courts and world opinion, much as a citizen places his trust in courts and the law of the land rather than resorting to his own rifle.

Figueres was no pacifist. He rose to power by leading a bloody revolution. In the years ahead he would participate in dozens of schemes to assassinate Nicaragua's Anastasio Somoza, and his son would fight for the Sandinistas with his blessing. He would even run guns to Castro in Cuba to help get rid of Batista. "I loved fighting," he exclaimed to a reporter for *National Geographic* in 1981, exploding the "peaceful Costa Rica" theme. "War is something you can be enthusiastic about!"[4]

But to his mind a standing army represented a threat, not a protection, when it came to democracies. I'll grant you, he would say, that the free world needed armies to defeat Hitler. I'll grant you that armies have their place. But they can be formed at will, they don't have to become constant parasites on the body politic just because they may be needed at some point in the future when diplomacy fails. He would draw an analogy to a physician: When your child is sick, it is crucially important that the doctor make a house call. But that doesn't mean he has to live with you all your life.

It was a point he would stress time and time again. And Costa Ricans were receptive to the message, particularly when it became clear that without an army's drain of resources, the national standard of living could climb higher and faster than that of any other nation in Central America. The analysis would become ingrained in the political platform of Don Pepe's followers, so much so that the following words, spoken by Oscar Arias in 1987, could have been said by Figueres in 1948: "The military in Latin America's main objective has been to preserve the status quo, and defend the privileged minorities, not necessarily defend their countries from foreign threat."

Of course, it was easier for Figueres to outlaw an army he had just defeated and decimated, an army to which he had no political or emotional ties. But then again, virtually every other leader faced with the same situation used it as a fine opportunity to reward supporters with guns and jobs, building an armed institution loyal to himself. The momentum such institutions develop over time is inevitable and frightening, leading ever-increasing budgets and a constant, subtle pressure to consider a military alternative—to make use of all those men and all that hardware just lying around. And that is the benign form of militarism, militarism under control. At worst, coups are the order of the day.

To avoid this, to make sure the military was abolished in fact as well as name, Figueres established a policy that high-level police appointments would shift with the government. They were political appointees, possessing no independent power base. A commander in one government could become a lowly guardsman in the next or be gone from the force entirely. Sergeants, what you might call midlevel career police bureaucrats, do not exist in Costa Rica. And members of the Rural or Civil Guard, as the two police branches are called, have no great status in the society.

These were the moments of vision, coupled with a farmer's pragmatism, that rearranged Costa Rica. In November 1949, 834 laws and decrees later, Figueres made good on his promise, turning the government over to Ulate.

Over the next four years, Figueres set about building a true political party at home, an organization beyond a cult of personality that would reach into the countryside, recruit new leaders, organize neighborhoods, and deliver the vote on election days. It was called Partido Liberación Nacional, the National Liberation Party. To see the party as akin to the Democratic party of the Roosevelt/Truman years would be accurate, both in terms of philosophy and political power. Figueres and his compatriots would do their jobs so well that the party would become the dominant force in Costa Rican politics to this day, a cultural as well as political coalition. Indeed, one of the basic ways of defining a person in Costa Rica is to ask whether he or she is *liberación* or *anti-liberación*. Many a young man has entered the ranks of the party, perhaps with political dreams, perhaps to hang out at the party's local club with friends, and worked his way up the ranks to a prominent governmental position. The latest, best-known product of the process is Arias.

But back in 1953, the first job of Liberación was to win

an election. With Figueres as a standard-bearer, there was little doubt of success. Don Pepe carried 65 percent of the vote and his coattails were long enough to usher in nearly two-thirds of the Costa Rican Congress as well. Although some supporters of Calderón (who was still in exile) boycotted the election, there was absolutely no doubt about the honesty of the process. The Supreme Election Tribunal, with the power of an independent branch of government, kept tight controls on the balloting, going so far as to order all police officers to remain inside their barracks. Even with bars closed, as decreed by law, election day became a national party, a celebration of civility. The Second Republic was on its way.

Figueres's four-year term as president was not nearly as dramatic as his eighteen-month term as head of the junta. There were some major breakthroughs, however. In 1954, the government negotiated a new contract with United Fruit that promised that 35 percent of the company's profits would return to Costa Rican coffers and that housing, schools, and medical facilities would revert to Costa Rican control. It was a precedent-setting agreement, making Costa Rican banana-pickers the highest-paid in the region and raising them almost to the middle-class status that was Don Pepe's aspiration for everyone. Meanwhile, he pushed forward a low-cost national housing program to fulfill another mainstay promise of the Liberación platform.

Such changes require the heavy hand of government, but it was Figueres's vision of socialism and capitalism tied to the guarantee of basic human rights that made his approach unique. He said it most simply in a small book he wrote while president, during the Christmas break between 1955 and 1956. Only one of dozens of pamphlets and essays he would write during his life, "Cartas a un

Ciudadano" (Letters to the Citizenry) covered topics rang-
ing from the most weighty philosophy to questions about
why government officials drive around in public cars. In a
section about his vision of government, Figueres tried to
explain the middle ground he was groping toward, somewhere between the United States and the Soviet Union:
"Socialism, as an economic doctrine, never has to be seen
as linked to totalitarian politics, that is to say, with des-
potism. And capitalism, in theory, absolute free enterprise, doesn't have to be related to colonial exploitation."5
    Meanwhile, there had just been another test of the ar-
myless republic's ability to withstand external pressure. In
January 1955, Costa Rica was invaded yet again from Nicaragua. This time, it was the son of the former president,
Teodoro Picado, the so-called puppet of Calderón, who
was in charge of the troops. The younger Picado had been
a classmate of Anastasio Somoza's son at West Point, although the military operation certainly didn't reveal strategic genius. The invaders traveled the historic route
south, reaching as far as Quesada, and even used a few
planes to strafe Costa Rican cities. They then took to the
radio airwaves, transmitting messages urging Costa Ricans
to rise up and overthrow Figueres, whom they said was a
Communist. The invaders called themselves "the Authentic Anti-Communist Revolutionary Army."
    If they really expected a popular uprising, they pro-
foundly misread the Costa Rican public. Figueres remained calm, calling on the Organization of American
States (OAS) to come to the country, analyze the situation,
and mediate the conflict. In effect he was calling on the
international policeman, the world tribunal, just as he had
said he would when he abolished the army. Sure enough,
the OAS expressed outrage, the United States backed

Costa Rica with moral support as well as a few planes to counter the air strikes from the north, and the invasion fizzled away to nothing. Not only were very few lives lost, but the sovereignty of the country, despite no military structure, was strengthened.

Figueres was not blameless in the matter of this mini-invasion. For years he had backed Nicaraguan revolutionaries who were intent on assassinating Somoza. Don Pepe made no bones about his hatred of Somoza, of dictatorship. In the coming years he would applaud "those boys, the Sandinistas" for carrying on the next generation's struggle against another Somoza. Perhaps he was even tempted to take up Somoza's challenge in 1954, when the Nicaraguan dictator suggested that the two meet at the border, pistols in hand, and fight it out man to man. Given that A. C. Sandino, the resistance fighter the Sandinistas are named for, was treacherously murdered at the bargaining table during peace negotiations, Figueres was probably wise to turn down the offer. "Grow up," his return note to Somoza reportedly read.

Flipping the coin over, there is Figueres's fascinating relationship with Fidel Castro and the Cuban Revolution. Again, it was his disdain of dictators, his belief in populism and self-determination, that led Figueres to support Castro's fight against Batista with what some saw as a crucial shipment of weapons during the last year of Figueres's first presidency, 1958. Castro recognized the import of the contribution and once he was firmly in power invited Don Pepe to join in a massive celebration of the victory of the revolution, July 26, 1961, in Havana. Enrique Carreras, a Figueres intimate, accompanied the ex-president on the trip and remembers that Figueres was asked to address a throng of almost five hundred thousand Cubans in the main square of the city.

But Figueres did not like what he was seeing, an emerging dictatorship of the left rather than the right and an intimate alliance with the Soviet Union. And so, ever blunt, ever the Catalán, Figueres took the microphone and, as Carreras remembers, began his speech with words to this effect:

"I'm hearing a lot of anti-United States expressions here, and a vocabulary that is not much in accord with our Occidental values. I want to warn you, you could be going down a path of no return, which will create a lot of hardship and sacrifice for the Cuban people." The United States has to be approached with the recognition that it dominates this hemisphere, Figueres pushed on, and can be a force for good, not necessarily evil.

The speech bombed. In fact, in a manner reminiscent of the untimely conclusion of the famous radio broadcast in 1942, a Cuban labor leader grabbed the microphone away. Although Figueres was allowed to finish, the Costa Rican delegation was quickly ushered to their hotel. The following morning, as Carreras puts it, "we were cordially invited to leave the country."

It would be twenty-one years before Castro invited Figueres to return to Costa Rica. There had been some prophecy in Don Pepe's comments in the early 1960s but that was not the subject of the meeting of June 1982. The Sandinistas, with strong Cuban support, had been in power for almost three years. The Nicaraguan border with Costa Rica was very hot, and it looked like war could break out. Figueres, Costa Rica's elder statesman yet sympathetic to the Sandinistas, ostensibly was in Cuba to hear from Castro about the United States' abuse of power and how to resolve that conflict.

Although two decades had passed, Carreras was with Figueres once again. He remembers that Castro was warming to his subject in his eloquent, long-winded, and relentless way, when Figueres showed that the years had not changed his personality. Carreras remembers Don Pepe stopping Castro "in a very strong tone" to say: "Listen, if you want to understand Costa Rica, realize that we are not only the most pro-Yankee people in Latin America, but probably the most pro-Yankee people in the world. Even more than England." And Figueres used that word *Yankee* advisedly, Carreras remembers, used it twice in fact, because Castro had employed the word derogatorily about the United States. "Fidel was shocked," Carreras continued. "He couldn't hide it, and he hides things very well." The Costa Rican delegation half expected to be sent packing yet again, but they weren't. And war with Nicaragua was averted more through Costa Rican diplomacy than Cuban intervention.

The amazing thing is that Figueres simply refused to be categorized. When then Vice-President Richard Nixon made his famous trip to Latin America in the late 1950s, to be spit upon by anti-U.S. demonstrators, Don Pepe all but defended the action. "People cannot spit on a foreign policy," he told a congressional subcommittee in Washington in 1958. "When American boys have been dying [in Korea], your mourning has been our mourning. When *our* people die, you speak of investments. Then you wonder why we spit."[6] Meanwhile, just to make sure no stereotype would hold him, during these same years Figueres had been actively soliciting CIA money to help organize political action in Central America. Looking back on it, in 1981, he told a *New York Times* reporter, "I was a good friend of Allen Dulles, who as you know had a very stupid brother, John Foster. Anyway, the CIA's cultural department helped me finance a magazine and some youth conferences here. But I never participated in espionage. I did beg them not to carry out the Bay of Pigs invasion of Cuba, which was madness, but they ignored me."[7]

Don Pepe's recollection is not to be fully trusted. Although the bulk of the CIA funding probably was for political journalism, no doubt Figueres was involved in intrigues bordering on "espionage," since he was bent on the overthrow of other governments. The CIA wanted Castro; it so happened that Don Pepe was more interested in Rafael Trujillo in the Dominican Republic and Somoza in Nicaragua. Exactly how all the money was spent (through various funnels it reached six figures) has never been explained.

What's more, in a superb political biography of Figueres, Charles Ameringer makes it quite clear that Don Pepe had no idea of the Bay of Pigs invasion before the fact. He felt left out, depressed, and even betrayed. He had expected Kennedy, as a young, liberal U.S. president, to treat him with respect. It wasn't so bad that the United States might try to overthrow Castro; that was understandable. It was that Figueres didn't know about it.

But of course, during that time he wasn't even the president of the country. Allowed to serve one four-year term, Don Pepe left office in 1958, only to see a coalition of anti-Liberación parties pull together to get their candidate elected president. Mario Echandi had no strength in Congress, however, and in 1962 one of Figueres's right-hand men during the revolution, Francisco Orlich, was elected president. A pattern was established, a national sense that a Liberación candidate would win the presidency every other election, while an anti-Liberación would rule in between.

This flip-flop no doubt was a response to unhappiness with the sitting government, but it also seemed to be the national way of avoiding a hardening of the arteries of either the bureaucracy or the police force. Make sure that people can still move, the voters seemed to say. What's more, it discouraged anyone from resorting to disruption and violence if the election went against them, because people strongly felt that if they waited four years, their party was going to be elected. And rumors of military coups were rife, particularly around 1962; declassified U.S. government documents from the Kennedy years show concern reached all the way to Washington. Yet democracy held, and this back-and-forth pattern continued all the way through the sixties and seventies (with one exception) and into the eighties, until underdog Oscar Arias, a Liberación man, won during an anti-Liberación year.

But back to Figueres. Quoted by John Kennedy as the Alliance for Progress was unveiled, asked for advice by Lyndon Johnson at the time the United States occupied the Dominican Republic, invited to teach a semester course on Latin America by Harvard University, Figueres rolled through the sixties. Even public revelations that he was a CIA agent didn't slow him down much. And as 1970 approached, a Liberación year for Costa Rican presidential politics, Don Pepe got the urge to run again. The constitution allowed him to do it, although the men of his generation would be the only ones allowed to serve more than four years. The party of his own creation certainly wouldn't stop him. And the opposition candidate Mario Echandi, the same man who had succeeded Figueres to the presidency in 1958, wasn't going to beat him. Don Pepe took 55 percent of the vote, as nearly 90 percent of the eligible voters went to the polls. It was, as people would soon chant in the United States, Four More Years.

The last time around for Figueres, his third in power, his second as president, is as difficult to categorize as the man himself. It was probably the least productive of his terms, but the most colorful and controversial. There were some achievements of substance: Despite a storm of protest, Figueres recognized the Soviet Union and allowed a Soviet embassy in San José. He also legalized Costa Rica's Communist party, the very same group he had outlawed two decades earlier, explaining that the Communists were like yeast in the bread—you need a little bit to make things rise, but too much destroys everything. He predicted that the party would never get more than a few percent of the popular vote, and to this day his prediction has held true.

To the people who argued that he was allowing the international Communist conspiracy to undermine and destabilize the country, Figueres mounted the same argument many times: Look, to see a monolithic Communist conspiracy lurking under every rug is a mistake. People are simply desperate by the millions, poor and starving. Don't waste time worrying about this so-called conspiracy—help the people who need help! All right, he would continue, let's even go so far as to say there is this conspiracy. So what? You defuse it with good public policy, with jobs and housing and opportunity. Now let's say there is no such conspiracy. So what? You still need good public policy.

Meanwhile, refusing to ignore Limón Province as so many politicians had done, Figueres made sure that the first highway linking the Atlantic to San José was finally pushed through. He also nationalized the Minor Keith railroad, which had become dangerously decrepit and unreliable.

With strong impetus from his second wife, Karen, and with a naturalist's vision that reached back to tree-planting days at La Lucha in the 1930s, Figueres made significant improvements and additions to the national park system. Costa Rica's public land holdings have become the most spectacular in Central America: Almost 10 percent of Costa Rican land is now under conservation and public control, a figure even higher than the United States. Figueres deserves much credit for this evolution.

And, finally, it was during these years that Figueres first began to talk about luring United States retirees to Costa Rica, offering tax benefits and other advantages to wealthy gringos approaching their golden years. It was a logical extension of his general attitude, which embraced North America both for himself and his country. It was the most open of open door policies. *Pensionados*, as the retirees are called, would take advantage of this largesse in increasing numbers, injecting dollars into the Costa Rican economy. U.S. corporations would take advantage as well, although whether they gave more than they took would become a hot political question at various times.

Then there was Robert Vesco, his version of taking advantage, and the shadow he cast on Figueres. Vesco arrived in Costa Rica in the middle of Figueres's term,

1972, keeping a few steps ahead of U.S. investigators who would soon charge him with stealing hundreds of millions of dollars in a mutual funds scam that involved foreign investments in United States enterprises. Vesco, who would become perhaps the world's most notorious international fugitive, holed up in the Bahamas before eventually settling in Cuba. In between, he stayed in Costa Rica as a friend and business associate of President Figueres.

The evidence that friendship veered into corruption was overwhelming, and damning. While Vesco came and went, his private plane reportedly avoided the usual customs searches at Juan Santamaría Airport. Moreover, Vesco had offered an unsecured loan of more than $2 million to a corporation associated with Figueres and La Lucha. When Vesco went on national radio to defend himself and his actions in Costa Rica, it turned out that the speech had basically been written by none other than Don Pepe. "Better I write his speeches than he write mine," said Figueres.[8] When Costa Rican investigators went to the Bahamas to follow Vesco's paper trail, they found a letter from Figueres himself, on official stationery, requesting the release of $60 million of Vesco's that the Bahamian government was holding. Meanwhile, Vesco's assets included a two-thousand-acre ranch in Guanacaste Province.

There was every appearance of outrageous, obvious corruption. Since everyone knew that Figueres had been having financial problems, including unpaid back taxes, suspicion deepened. The anti-Liberación press had a field day: "Don Dinero," they called Vesco. When United States requests to extradite Vesco were denied, the ruling made sense given the Costa Rican legal system but at the same time conveyed a strong impression that Figueres was sheltering Vesco from justice. Figueres even went so far as to stand in for Vesco at the wedding of Vesco's son, because Vesco would have been arrested had he returned to New Jersey for the ceremony.

Throughout it all, Don Pepe maintained a posture that would be difficult to translate into our political language. On the one hand, he seemed genuinely affronted and hurt that people accused him of corruption. His personal business dealings did not influence his public policy, he would argue. They were absolutely distinct matters. Meanwhile, the Vesco affair also triggered Figueres's stubborn streak, particularly when it came to loyalty. A cardinal rule associates have attributed to Figueres is: Once a friend, always a friend, no matter what. End of discussion. The rule included Vesco, though this does not mean that Figueres had no financial motives for dealing with Vesco, that the charges of using his public position for private gain were unfounded.

In fact, as the controversy swirled around him, Figueres watched Richard Nixon trying to deal with another controversy, Watergate, and simply could not understand how that man could jettison loyal followers like Ehrlichman and Haldeman. Disgusting, spineless, Figueres would say, adding that he had the speech that would save the Nixon presidency: All Nixon had to do was go on national television and explain to the American people how sometimes followers become overzealous, how organizations sometimes get out of control. People understand and forgive such things. But what you never do is sacrifice the people around you in order to save your own neck. "Bananagate," Figueres scoffed at his own problems, linking Vesco and Watergate.

Nixon couldn't survive Watergate, but Figueres survived Vesco. The association became a strong campaign issue, helping the anti-Liberación candidate win election in 1974, but it was the anti-Liberación's turn anyway. And there were so many wonderful achievements that people preferred to remember, and wonderful anecdotes, too: for example, how Don Pepe, while still president in the last term, sixty-five years old, grabbed a machine gun and raced down to the airport to confront the man who had hijacked a plane. (International reports said that Figueres personally shot out the tires of the jet to prevent it from leaving, which proved to be a slight exaggeration.) Or how he loved to travel, having his picture taken at Disney World with Mickey Mouse, then causing the Costa Rican Congress to balk at allowing him permission (as required by Costa Rican law) to return to Florida to watch a U.S. space shot at Cape Kennedy. He went anyway.

By 1982, when Don Pepe's old co-conspirator from 1948, Luis Alberto Monge, was elected president, Figueres was installed in the largely ceremonial role of roving ambassador. Rove he did. He returned to his ancestral roots in Spain to receive acclaim, then went to the Great Wall in China, donning a blue Mao jacket that he would often wear in later years, marveling at the incredible achievement the Great Wall represented. All this took place in the middle of Costa Rican negotiations with Taiwan over trade opportunities. "Insulting, insensitive, and embarrassing," stormed his detractors. In 1985, seventy-nine years old, he boarded a small boat at the wild border with Nicaragua to cross the San Juan River and meet Daniel Ortega. Figueres returned with Ortega's promise of free elections—a promise that was not fulfilled. In that same year, Don Pepe aired his views in the local weekly, *The Tico Times,* about the arrival of U.S. green berets in

Costa Rica, who were there, ostensibly, to help build roads and train civil guardsmen. "We don't want a group of jack-booted young men here goose-stepping, saluting and clicking their heels. This would mean the beginning of militarism in our country. I see in this another U.S. mistake in Latin America in the making." He felt hurt, he said, to have to criticize his friend the United States, but "the only way to deal with the so-called Communist danger in Latin America is to drown them in freedom and social well-being."[9]

Such remarks were controversial but generally accepted. When, at eighty years old, Figueres traveled to Managua to accept the Augusto Cesar Sandino Award from the Sandinista revolutionary government, the controversy was deeper and the gesture less appreciated. A month later, Figueres was forced to do something he rarely did—apologize in public. The reason was his response to a reporter who asked what he thought U.S. President Ronald Reagan's biggest mistake had been. "Having been born," said Figueres.

All of this might suggest that Figueres was "losing it," that his mental powers have ebbed over the past few years, and to some extent, this has been the case. Yet his personal flamboyance, as well as his stubborn embrace of the United States despite efforts to unseat its repressive puppets, were not marks of senility. They were the guiding impulses of his life.

And even in recent years, when Don Pepe has gathered people around him at La Lucha to discuss international affairs, there has been nothing outdated or demented about his analysis. Look, he has said, humanity is in a critical situation and Central America is at the heart of it. Central America and the Caribbean, if not properly handled, could be the place where the true war to end all wars will begin. This is like the Mediterranean, the new Mediterranean of humanity. Understand that it is always at the frontier, at the limit of empires, where superpowers clash. Our region has been that frontier for the Spanish, the Dutch, the British, the North Americans, even the Russians. And because for ten thousand years war has been seen as the ultimate, final extension of politics, everyone has to be very, very careful in Central America. Our thinking has not advanced as fast as the weapons. War is still the ultimate extension, but this time the war kills one and all.

These are certainly not the rantings of a confused old man. And if you need any more proof that Don Pepe Figueres has been a *caudillo,* a strong political force, right into the 1980s, then consider this: According to very good sources, Figueres had decided as late as 1986 that he was going to run for president one more time, with his old friend ex-president Oduber as vice-president. He would find a way around any legal prohibition, he told his supporters. He gathered all the strongest possible Liberación candidates together to tell them of his decision.

They did not laugh at the old man, nearly eighty years old, and his senile ambition. On the contrary, every one of them was willing to step aside, saying it was Don Pepe's right to run uncontested within the party if that's what he chose to do. There was only one who was as stubborn as Figueres, who would not be denied, who felt the next generation's time had come. Today, he is the president of Costa Rica.

But before one can understand Arias and his presidency, there is one more element of Don Pepe's legacy that needs to be explored, another vestige of the vision he brought to "this toy country," as he once called it. As fervently as Don Pepe embraced the United States, so has the United States's influence come to permeate Costa Rica in a variety of ways. Yes, Costa Rica is a Yankee-loving country, as Figueres told Castro. It's just that the Yankees who have come here have taken that to mean a free ticket to pursue every conceivable expression of the American dream, from live and let live to the freest of free enterprise, from left-wing pacifism to right-wing clandestine warfare.

INTERMEDIO DOS (SECOND INTERLUDE)

Strategic

I drove north through the heart of the country, on the eastern side of the big mountains, right up the middle, and in my search for United States influence all I had to do was look down at the asphalt. The roads are new and good, smooth as those across our own prairie. The whole north-central part of Coast Rica is opening up, suddenly accessible because international (read, U.S.) money has been pouring in for "infrastructure" over the past five years or so. Costa Ricans are grateful: They can be home in minutes by car instead of hours by horseback; they can move produce to market in hours by truck instead of days by ox cart. Land values are skyrocketing, new farms spring-ing to life. It is boom time.

Costa Ricans also think they understand why all the bridges along the highway were built with enough cement and reinforced steel to carry a couple of tanks: This road goes straight up to the Nicaraguan border before it stops. If it ever happened that United States troops stationed in Panama needed to get north in a hurry, they would now be able to sprint, fully equipped. And when the interna-tional (read, U.S.) agencies said they wanted to take satel-lite pictures of the region to show local farmers where the best grazing land for their cattle might be—well, people shrugged and smiled, because families who have spent generations working land usually don't need satellite pic-tures to tell them what's happening, although sometimes foreign military strategists do.

But there is one more step in optimistic Costa Rican thinking. As long as Costa Rica doesn't let itself get dragged into a war, as long as the border with Nicaragua is respected, as long as the Arias government stands firm about not letting the contras turn northern Costa Rica into a war zone, as long as the peace plan has a chance, then there is reason to hope that the military strategists will never need their road. They will go home, as North Americans tend to do, and what they leave behind will help Costa Ricans for decades to come. So maybe Costa Rican luck will hold: They can have their cake and eat it too, have their roads built for a tank and have peace.

My friend Rick Holland was riding shotgun, and I was glad to take advantage of his good company. Rick had been born in the States but arrived in Costa Rica with his parents as a young boy, attended local schools, married a

Costa Rican woman, and understood the north country because he had done some farming up there. His mother, Linda, is one of the nicest, best-informed people in the capital; if she doesn't know about something, it probably hasn't happened. Linda and her husband, Cliff, in their low-key, open-minded way, have probably welcomed and encouraged more foreign journalists and young expatriates in Costa Rica than anyone. What Rick knows and cares about most is land; if ever a person were meant to be an independent farmer, it is him. And in Costa Rica that dream is still possible.

We reached Ciudad Quesada before midday. It was a busy Friday, and Quesada is still full of a frontier, cowboy feeling, a town where the business of one man on a main street consists of making and selling cattle brands. It being Friday, the auction was in progress, big bulls, steers, and cows drawing somewhere around fifty colones a kilo, weighing maybe four hundred fifty kilos—an animal for 335 U.S. dollars. The auctioneer rattled through the rising numbers as fast in Spanish as they do in English. There were Brahmas with their big humps, Holsteins full of milk, and a hybrid of the two that gives both milk and meat. There were also plenty of buyers, each with his own brand. Surrounded by cattle the ranchers had learned to ignore their staring brown eyes. Between bids the men took breaks for hamburgers.

As we left town, headed north, everything felt so young, so new. Long rows of pineapple had been planted where huge forests had stood as little as ten years ago. There were also irrigation ditches and grazing land, citrus trees laden with fruit—the marks of hard effort and transformation, a heartland in the making, with a sense of urgency about it.

After about fifteen miles, ever closer to Nicaragua, we turned east near a cluster of buildings known as Muelle. Even this road was smooth, black asphalt heading toward the horizon, but it had a saw horse across the lanes and a *No Hay Paso* sign—Do Not Enter. We ignored it.

Watching the dirt roads on either side, wondering which to take, we asked a man resting on the porch of his home. "You just missed it," he said. "It's this one right here." Forget the slick asphalt, "this one" was dirt and rock. Well, that's what rental cars are for.

Bouncing and banging, we drove a long way on the rocky trail. The land opened up beautifully. The soil was very rich, plots under cultivation around small but comfortable-looking *fincas*. Goats, cows, chickens, and pigs all made appearances. Not much coffee, though it grows throughout most of Costa Rica, but pineapple, citrus, onions, yams, and plantains were abundant. There were no other cars on the road, which was good because the path only allowed for one at a time. A car was unusual enough to draw attention; women in the middle of weeding stood up to stare, then bent over their work. Children stuck knuckles in their mouths. Goats looked up, but didn't stop munching.

The road hooked, and then I had to slam on the brakes. A man on horseback was trotting toward us. His brown stallion was tall and handsome and wet around the legs. I saw why: A rapidly moving stream, maybe forty feet wide, had cut across the roadway. He explained that it wasn't as bad as it looked, that if you watched the water you could see where a shallower half-moon-shaped vestige of the road still remained. Well, that's what a rental car is for. "No matter what you do," said Rick, "once you get started, don't stop."

I didn't stop, and neither did the steam, which continued to sizzle off of the hot engine block until we were well past the stream. The road became more dirt, less rock, and then all of a sudden there was a wide open field. Acres of land were perfectly flat and covered with such nice green grass that it looked like rich felt on a giant pool table. But that image shredded on the barbed wire that ringed the man-made clearing. Parallel to that fence was another one maybe fifteen feet inside that appeared electrified.

A hundred yards farther on, a gate was adorned with those convex mirrors that allow people wide-angle views. A few guards were on duty, although no one seemed to be inside the low-slung building beyond the gate. And high above it all, rising up hundreds of feet, sporting little red lights that blinked on and off, were four transmitting towers arranged in a rectangle, with enough space between them for a good-sized airplane to land. What was being protected was the Voice of America at Altamirita, 50,000 watts strong, beaming messages into Nicaragua and, presumably, receiving messages as well.

The Voice of America began transmission on January 15, 1985, when the clandestine war along the Nicaraguan border was at its hottest. From the beginning people questioned the location because they thought the mountains would effectively cut the range of the signal into Nicaragua. But broadcasting propaganda might not be the only function of as sophisticated a communications system as this, located on a long dirt road in the middle of rural northern Costa Rica. There was also some fear among the families in the area about whom the towers might attract. By and large, however, people looked on the bright side. The former owners of the land had got what they considered to be an eminently fair price. Locals were hired at decent wages (the equivalent of about two hundred dollars a month) to help smooth the land and build the towers. And many sturdy tools were brought to the site—hammers, shovels, saws, screwdrivers—with some eventually finding their way into the local community. So it wasn't an altogether bad thing by any stretch.

But it certainly was an eerie, twenty-first-century technology bristling out of a remote, pastoral nook. We turned around before the late afternoon rains made the stream yet wilder, and I found myself thinking about the word *remote*. Throughout history, places that once were "remote" had suddenly become "strategic," and people who'd asked for little more than good rain and sun in the right measure suddenly became engulfed in violence far beyond their control.

We made it back to the highway, but there was one more visit we had to make. We banged and bounced down another long dirt road, this one snaking up a good-sized hill, until we reached a village called Palmera at the crest of a ridge. After going a little farther and a little higher, we pulled into a dirt driveway. My shoes were muddy, so I left them on the porch of the Gamboa family's home and stepped inside.

The house was typical of a hard-working rural campesino family, a farmer's home. It was well-built, well-finished, and painted, with an intricately carved wood-beamed ceiling, comfortable furniture, room enough for three generations, warm lights, and good spirits. It was above all else a congenial place. Two grown sons, Ricardo and Edgar, talked with their friend Rick about what they had planted. Their father, José Maria, wanted to hear what people in San José were saying about Arias, since he rarely got to the capital himself.

125

He was told the new tax plan had people upset. His wife appeared with a pitcher of milk straight from their cows and took her seat near a wall hanging that thanked God for all the ways in which the mother of the house was so supportive and loving. Her grown daughter, with bright eyes and a quick smile, wondered if we'd heard the story about their truck yet. No, not yet, we said.

Well, said the father, it seems as though one of the sons had the family's good truck and was driving down a back road a few nights earlier when a cow suddenly appeared. There was no time to stop, nowhere to swerve, and the truck plowed straight into that cow. Until something like that happens to you, there's no way to appreciate just how big and strong cows are. When your truck hits one, you don't dent a fender, you destroy the front end.

Now, letting a cow stray, letting him get onto the road at night, is a major mistake people in a rural community sometimes make. The Gamboas found out who owned the cow and were not surprised to hear it was an absentee situation, the guy was the general manager of the swankiest San José hotel and has a finca up in the hills. The insurance would cover most of the repairs, the Gamboas figured, but there was the deductible, and they expected the hotel manager to ante up. They planned to write a letter and send it off the next day.

After we heard the story, Señora Gamboa insisted we eat a little something before making the dark drive toward Quesada, and so we had some *bocas,* the Costa Rican term for late afternoon hors d'oeuvres. The talk moved around the table, and I thought about the accident: For starters, this family not only has a good truck, but it's not the end of the world when their good truck hits a cow and is put out of commission. No one will lose his land, no one will starve. Papa is not screaming at his boy, let alone smacking him for running into a cow. There's insurance, and the insurance will cover it. What's more, the guy who owned the cow could be a neighbor, or he could be the biggest bigwig in San José—he still owes what the insurance won't pay because it was his cow in the road, and this family feels it has every right to expect payment from him. There is no fearfulness, no sense that social status or financial position would interfere with justice. A so-called lowly rural farmer has every right to make demands on a San José businessman.

There, I thought, are some Costa Rican strengths.

We stood up to go, bid farewell with kisses and *hasta luegos*, and I put on my muddy shoes. But before driving off, Rick and I took one more walk. It was nostalgia for him, a breath of fresh air for me. The dark road moved through farmland with pineapples here, big ornamental plants there, until it reached the side of the ridge. The moon was partly obscured by clouds, so we could barely see the valley below, silvery, peaceful, wide and long, stretching toward dim mountains in the distance. Electric lights twinkled. The fertility and tranquility were almost palpable.

Yet at the edge of the view there was a red gleam blinking with a beat all its own where the four tall towers stood.

CHAPTER SIX

Transplanted Farmers

The most incredible thing about Costa Rica's small contingent of U.S. farmers from the Midwest on the one hand and its small contingent of U.S. farmers from Fairhope, Alabama, on the other is not how different expatriates can be.

True, these two North American presences in northern Costa Rica are just about as far apart politically, religiously, emotionally, and ethically as people can be. One group is personified by a right-wing war-pilot Indiana farmer turned CIA operative, who has handled money, supplies, and possibly guns and drugs for the contra war against Nicaragua. The other group is personified by a pacifist, draft-resisting, nature-loving cooperative cheese-maker, an Alabama Quaker whose primeval cloud forest has attracted environmentalists the world over.

Yet the truly amazing aspect of their stories is how they both can express, almost word for word, the exact same motives for coming to Costa Rica, the same lure and attraction that made them single out this country from all of Latin America as the place to make a new beginning.

Both groups are products of Don Pepe's open door policy to the United States. Their experiences have come to symbolize American dreams (or perhaps nightmares) transplanted. And both, in profoundly different ways, have deeply influenced recent life and times in Costa Rica.

First, meet John Hull, the dean of expatriate midwestern farmers. In his mid sixties, leathery-skinned, bald, and hard-headed, with broad, flat features like the land he came from, Hull sits in his handsome, airy ranch house overlooking a green tributary of the San Juan River, about thirty miles south of Nicaragua. He recalls how he wound up in this little corner of nowhere. It was the late 1950s, early 1960s. His years as a World War II fighter pilot were long over and he had returned to his farm in Indiana. He and his father decided to look around outside the United States for a little place to have an adventure, make an investment, maybe even put down a few roots.

"So, we took our airplane," Hull remembers, "and a soil-testing kit. We flew to every country in Central and South America. We were looking for a friendly, peaceful country, with nice people and good, rich soil." They hunted and fished their way around the continent, "had a big helluva time," and when all was said and done, Hull settled on Costa Rica.

And now, meet Wilfred Guindon, known as Wolf, a fitting point man for the Alabama Quakers. He looks like a beardless Pete Seeger with a hard hat on his head and a machete in his hand, cutting a trail through one of the last remaining cloud forests in Central America—a preserve his effort has helped protect. If ever the word *verdant* applied to a place, this is it; even the water from the trees and moss seems to drip green. Wisps and then banks of clouds rush over the high ridge, carrying mist so thick that Guindon almost disappears. Then the gray departs, revealing mountain views of yet more green.

Wolf lives in a place of his making called Monteverde, Green Mountain. As the crow flies he is not many miles south of John Hull's ranch, although these are different worlds, and no roads connect the two. Lean, dressed in blue jeans splattered with mud, handling his machete like a carpenter handles a hammer, Wolf has memories of Costa Rica that stretch back even farther than Hull's.

The year was 1948, and the United States had begun its first peacetime draft. That didn't sit well with Guindon, nor with other young men who belonged to the same Quaker meeting in Fairhope, Alabama. So they sent polite letters to their draft board explaining why they were refusing to sign up. And the four of them were sentenced to jail terms of a year and a day. "Jail?" says Wolf, hacking at the dense underbrush with his machete, "that was a lark. It was easy time."

But when they got out, with time off for good behavior, a refrain they had heard often rang in their ears: If you don't want to fight for this country, you ought to leave it. Not a bad idea, they began to think, especially with all this militarism and Red Menace talk in the air. And so the Alabama Quakers sent a delegation touring through Central and South America, stopping to talk with people in every country. They were looking for a friendly, peaceful nation, with nice people and good, rich soil for farming. By 1950, they had found a place that not only met every criterion but had actually had the courage and vision to abolish its army two years earlier. That sealed it—Costa Rica.

Now back to John Hull. When he found his piece of real estate up north, he brought a farmer's mentality to the jungle. The soil-testing kit told him the dirt was great, but first he had to clear out dense forest to get to it. There were no roads, no electricity. "I hired fifty guys for three years chopping down jungle," Hull remembers. "They'd get it down to about six inches, chopped it with machetes, and then we'd sprig in grass." There was huge timber on the land, magnificent mahogany and hardwood trees the likes of which haven't been seen in the United States for generations, which he could sell to sawmills. Land and labor were so cheap that the wood alone recouped half the cost of the project. Hull saw himself as a pioneer, squarely in the tradition of the men who moved across the American plains, beating back the elements to make secure, prosperous lives for themselves amid the wilderness.

The Alabama contingent didn't have the luxury of a small airplane to get them to Costa Rica. Besides, they weren't a one-man operation. By November 1950, seven Quaker families had banded together to make the trip, selling everything they owned and loading a truck and trailer with household goods to begin their trek to the New World. William Penn, the Colonial Quaker whose New World came to be called Pennsylvania, would have understood perfectly what they were doing, and why.

Some people went ahead to San José to wait, while hardier members of the group tried to get the vehicles down the ribbon of road that has never lived up to its grand name of the Pan-American Highway. After the road crossed from Mexico into Guatemala, it petered out to nothing. The group managed to load onto a flatbed railroad car for two hundred miles, then back on a road to inch through Nicaragua. When they reached the border of Costa Rica on Christmas Day, 1950, they found that for all practical purposes, the road ended. There were two choices: Turn around, or build a road through the jungle. They chose to build, following creek beds and trails, fashioning bridges out of trees and a corduroy road out of anything at hand. It would take them a month to travel the next twelve miles through the jungle.

Once all the Quakers were united in San José, they set out in search of land. They had come from farming and dairy country in Alabama and figured they would continue to farm in Costa Rica. After six months of looking around, carefully weighing pros and cons, knowing that they wanted to be high enough in the mountains to avoid malaria, which still infested the lowlands, they found Monteverde, the Green Mountain. The group bought three thousand acres at roughly twenty-five dollars an acre and received a mixture of high pasture land and mountains, remote and beautiful. "We came here to be at the end of the road," says Wolf, laughing from his perch in the cloud forest because even the bone-jarring dirt road up the mountain stopped a few miles back. "We're not the evangelical Quakers, not the aggressive kind."

John Hull's dreams were more aggressive, but they also came true. Over the course of a decade, thousands of acres of jungle were cleared by Costa Rican laborers under Hull's management, revealing open ranges for cattle and fertile soil for pineapples and oranges. His house took shape, a wide open breezeway between symmetrical buildings. Electricity and water were brought to the site high above the river. Hull began a second family with a Costa Rican wife. Remote as the hacienda was, a smooth grass strip allowed the plane to come and go; instead of many hours on horseback, travel could be accomplished in minutes through the air. Soon official aviation maps of Costa Rica would show the runway, named simply "John Hull."

As Hull made periodic trips back to Indiana to check on his holdings there, he spread the gospel about Costa Rica. He was evangelical, you might say. Times being tough for farmers in the Midwest, the lure of the Costa Rican frontier was strong. Before long a handful of farmers in the area, some from Indiana, some from across the border in Illinois, bought up hunks of land to follow in Hull's footsteps. He would manage the properties for a fee, or maybe for a percentage of ownership. Tens of thousands of acres became involved, "six to eight airstrips," says Hull. A man like Jim Denby, whose son raced motorcycles in Indiana with Hull's grandson, bought in. His friend Frank Bellm, Hull's associate Bill Crone, and a Vietnam veteran named Bruce Jones were also among the arrivals. They were attracted by the timber and opportunity of farming, by freedom to do what they wanted on a new frontier. They formed "one big family," as Jim Denby would tell a reporter from *The State Journal Register* newspaper of central Illinois.[10] And they had politics in common: They were all solid, maybe even rabid, anti-Communists, rock-ribbed rightwing.

At Monteverde, subsistence farming, more than creating surplus for profit, was the dream. The land was divided among the handful of families amounting to forty-four people. A small church was knocked together where the Quakers could hold religious services. These consist of an hour of meditation on Sundays during which anyone is allowed to speak whatever comes to mind. New England-style town meetings became the forum for community decisions.

One of the first of those decisions was perhaps the most important of all: About one thousand acres of forest near the top of the mountain overlooking Monteverde would be left alone. This was not the result of some kind of prophetic group vision, a premonition that such a place would soon become as precious as gold. Rather, it was a simple realization that the forests protected the crucial headwaters of the rivers that coursed to the valley below and that the forests were a part of the natural harmony that brought rain to the surrounding lands. "We came in as developers," says Wolf. "We were always looking for a place to cut trees that wouldn't affect the headwaters. Problem was, the more we understood, the more we realized that we were always affecting it, directly or indirectly."

A much more immediate realization for the Quakers was that subsistence farming was not going to give them the hard cash they needed to buy all the essentials they couldn't grow. They put their heads together, called on their dairy farming experience, and decided to start a cheese factory. With a 200-gallon vat, a secondhand boiler, and some old Quaker Oats cans (appropriately enough) for molds, the first week's production yielded 350 pounds. By the early 1980s, the factory was turning out two tons a day, employing fifty people at excellent wages, buying the equivalent of seventy thousand dollars of milk each month from local dairy farmers, and providing much of the domestic cheese in Costa Rica. It is run as a cooperative.

To hear John Hull tell it, he would have been happy on his ranch, having picked the right place and worked hard to choose the right time, except that those damned Communists fomenting revolution in Nicaragua got wind of him. The year was 1978, or early 1979, "forget asking me about dates and years, I'm terrible at them," Hull apologizes. "It was when Carter set up the deal to overthrow Somoza." Historical analysis aside, Hull remembers PB-54 amphibian planes and DC-3s "flying arms from Panama and Havana, flying right into Liberia. It was an open operation. No way an operation like that can be carried out without the approval of the United States Intelligence and the Costa Rican government."

The Sandinistas, Hull says, knew that he controlled a number of small airstrips near the border. They approached him, "and wanted to use the strips as staging areas. Now I'd talked to them, seen their camps, and there was always a hard-core Communist element to them. It was clear even to a dumb U.S. rancher like me. So I said no. And they put me on their hate list."

Hull's assessment of himself as "a dumb U.S. rancher" is too self-effacing. Aside from the obvious fact that dumb U.S. ranchers don't find themselves observing Sandinista military camps in the middle of a revolution, Hull also acknowledged in a 1987 interview in *The Wall Street Journal* that his father, whom he admired, was a military intelligence man as early as World War I and remained in intelligence even when he settled into farming in Indiana. During the Depression, Hull said, his father infiltrated labor meetings, reporting the names of "reds" to the government. "I'd say it's somewhat the same situation I've

135

got here," Hull told the *Journal*. "He'd pass along information."[11] Exactly when Hull began to pass information to the CIA, via the U.S. embassy in San José, is difficult to say. Most likely it began during the Reagan years, although it could have preceded 1980.

In any event, John Hull had not only carved out the right place and time for himself but for the CIA as well. He welcomed the opportunity to be the eyes and ears for the agency, to "fight Communists" much like his father before him. As money and pressure poured into the area to combat the victorious Sandinistas, John Hull found himself in the thick of intrigues that often involved death.

Back at Monteverde, the variety of life, not death, was at issue. When most Costa Ricans hear "los Cuaqueros," the Quakers, they still think of cheese, but there was a growing band of international naturalists who associated the Monteverde Quakers with conservation in general and a unique animal in particular. That animal is *bufo periglenes*, better known as the golden toad.

It was one of the teenagers in the Quaker community who first found a golden toad twenty-odd years ago. The creature is shaped like the average toad but so bright—red actually—that it glows in the dark green of the forest. Startled researchers, among them a graduate student from California named George Powell, realized that the cloud forest of Monteverde harbored other animals that exist in only a few places in the world. Powell could see that cloud forests and tropical forests everywhere were being cleared and destroyed at a devastating rate and he urged the Quakers at Monteverde to expand what, simply by good instinct, they had preserved. It didn't take all that much to move people like Wolf Guindon in that direction.

Meanwhile, the golden toad, captured so beautifully on

color film in magazines like *National Geographic*, became an international celebrity. Like the little snail darter in Tennessee, which stopped a huge dam, the toad aroused sympathy and came to symbolize all things that need to be saved from destruction. It was an endangered species that inspired affection as well as donations.

For John Hull, neither toads nor some wet trees needed saving, but a way of life did, and the destroyers were the Communists in Managua. Hull believes the Communists have their tentacles everywhere. "Our government is infiltrated in the States, and evidently this government here [in Costa Rica] is too."

Around 1982 Hull was approached by six men, Nicaraguans, who had come to believe that the Sandinistas had betrayed the promise of the revolution against Somoza. "They wanted to set up an operation against the Sandinistas," says Hull. "They wanted to bring wounded here and get them to hospitals." In effect, they were asking to use the airstrips Hull controlled, much as the Sandinistas had asked three years earlier. This time, Hull agreed. These were anti-Communists, after all, who would come to be known variously as contras, or freedom fighters. Among the group were Edén Pastora (the infamous Nicaraguan Commandante Zero, whom neither the Sandinistas nor the CIA could control) and Hugo Spadafora, "the guy who got his head cut off," as Hull puts it (the man's head was indeed found in a U.S. mailbag in Costa Rica in September 1985; his body had been floating in a river near the Panama border). "Of course I'm using names," Hull continues, "but it's like the CIA; you don't know anybody's name."

Actually, for a long time Hull denied any involvement with the CIA, although by 1987 he did come around to admitting that money and help had been funneled his way. They would come to his ranch, he says: "CIA guys don't pull out passports and say, 'I'm Joe Blow of the CIA,' but they identified themselves. They came out and gave me advice on how to beef up security. I did believe there would be an assassination attempt against my life." Guards and walkie-talkies became a part of everyday life. Throughout it all, to this day, Hull insists that his efforts were strictly "humanitarian." The airstrips "were never used for gunrunning," he claims.

From the halls of Congress in Washington to the jails of San José, people would dispute that claim. Indeed, even other members of Hull's "big family" of transplanted midwestern farmers would contradict the dean. Jim Denby, for example, told *The State Journal Register* in early 1984 that he had "about 1,000 contras" living on his farm with him. They would cross the river for raids against the Sandinistas, then return to the safety of "neutral" Costa Rican soil. "It's a 9 to 5 war," said Denby at the time.[12] Almost four years later, Denby's small plane would be shot down over Nicaragua. He was held by the Sandinistas for eight weeks on charges of aiding the contras, then released.

Meanwhile, another member of the "family," Bruce Jones, allowed a reporter from *Life* magazine to hang around during 1984, taking pictures and conducting interviews. The result was an article in *Life* in February 1985 titled "A CIA Man in Nicaragua." Jones was described as "a soldier working with the CIA," explaining that he had trained contras and led them into battle. As Jones remembered, in May of 1982 CIA shipments including antiaircraft guns began arriving at airstrips on Costa Rican farms after dark. "We'd know the date the planes were coming and wait for them," Jones told *Life*, estimating that one hundred such trips were made in a two-year period.

It strains credibility that John Hull had no idea all this was going on. He was managing these farms, after all. Yet it also strains credibility that CIA operatives would talk so openly about their work. Jones, having violated Costa Rica's neutrality laws, fled the country just as the magazine hit the stands. "He couldn't have been more stupid," contra leader Alfonso Robelo said to the Costa Rican press. "He's a show-off, letting them take pictures."[13] And Hull, his public profile growing ever bigger, nevertheless remained accessible to the American press. "Come on in, let's see what I can talk you out of," he said to me as late as December 1987, when I arrived unannounced and uninvited at the doorstep of his remote ranch.

The best explanation of such obvious incongruity, such a surreal mixture of secrecy and openness, is that these farmers are not the well-trained CIA men we read about in spy novels (and who no doubt exist). They were there to be used—and welcomed the opportunity. They were amateur operatives with a homemade "cover." They had political and psychological motives for playing at war. And their remote corner of the world suddenly had become "strategic"—just as the 50,000-watt Voice of America towers, broadcasting less than ten miles from Hull's ranch, suggested.

But none of that proves that these men kept their hands clean in dealing with what had quickly become a very dirty little war. In fact, many things suggest the opposite. For example, Rob Owen, who worked under Oliver North as a messenger during the time North was secretly sending money to the contras in violation of congressional prohibitions, testified to Congress that Hull was receiving ten thousand dollars a month to be given to one contra group.

"Ridiculous," Hull called such reports in the Costa Rican *Tico Times* back in June 1986.[14] By May 1987, in *The Wall Street Journal*, his comment changed to, "I've got receipts for every penny of it."[15]

While the ex-station chief for the CIA reportedly was refering to Hull as the CIA's main man in northern Costa Rica, and later admitting that Hull's airstrip was used in apparently illegal weapons shipments, there were periodic big meetings at the ranch house itself. One, Hull recounted to *The Wall Street Journal*, involved Edén Pastora and Alfonso Robelo. Pastora, once a Sandinista, then a contra, was unwilling to join forces with a bunch of contras who used to be Somoza's men, the very people he had fought against in the revolution. The Sandinistas had gone bad, he said, but still Somoza had been a tyrant and he would not fight alongside those men. Both the CIA (perhaps through Hull) and Robelo were pressuring Pastora to come in under one umbrella. If you don't, they warned, the CIA will cut off all support to you. Despite the ultimatum, Pastora refused and left by boat to return to the Nicaraguan border.

Meanwhile, the meetings Wolf Guindon and the Quakers were hosting were of another sort entirely. By 1972, they had made their first purchase of additional cloud-forest land around Monteverde, abutting the thousand acres they had set aside in the 1950s. By 1984, the preserve was up to 8,600 acres. But to make it work, the Costa Ricans who lived nearby had to understand and support what was happening. Without that support, poachers could cut down the forest and squatters, by Costa Rican law, could lay claim to open land simply by moving in and staying put for several years. A tedious grass-roots education process took place, night after night of community gatherings to explain the goals and reasons for a nature preserve. "It's been something of a hassle," says Wolf. As lumber gets scarcer and the price keeps rising, the short-term financial benefits of clearing the forest are only that much more tempting. "All this water here will be diverted for hydroelectric projects and irrigation down below," Guindon adds. "So the next generation will really appreciate this. But this generation doesn't because you're not letting them clear the forest."

Both the locals and the Costa Rican government have gotten the message. Costa Ricans now work in the park and by and large respect and protect its boundaries. The government has offered tax breaks and other incentives to the Quakers, which has helped them keep ahead of the lumbermen; between 1984 and 1987 the amount of forest under their control had doubled again, to 16,000 acres. The goal is a 27,000-acre park, held in private hands but subject to all the laws against logging of any national park. "Costa Rica has paid a lot of attention to the Quakers," says President Arias. "We have supported and will support the Quakers in Monteverde."

John Hull had been having problems with squatters, too, who would move in on one or another of the farms he was managing while the owners were back in the Midwest. Most people see land-squatting confrontations around Costa Rica as a sign that the Costa Rican ideal of a small farm for everyone is in jeopardy, but Hull has a different explanation. "These squatters are 100 percent backed by Communists," he says. "This is strictly a destabilization effort run by the Communists. It costs us four hundred to five hundred dollars to get an eviction, and it takes six weeks to get the guy out. The eviction's good for twenty-eight days, and on the twenty-ninth day, they're back. On one farm we had eleven evictions in two years."

Regardless, Hull had much bigger problems on his hands than squatters. Less than a month after the meeting between Pastora and Robelo broke up in bitterness, as the CIA threat that Pastora had better play ball or be cut out of the action was still in the air, Pastora held a jungle press conference just over the Costa Rican border in Nicaragua to explain his side of the situation. The place was called La Penca. It was May 1984, and about two dozen journalists traveled from San José to cover the event. That night, without warning, a bomb with two to four pounds of C-4 plastic explosives ripped through the camp. Pastora was injured but survived. Three of the journalists did not, and others sustained injuries including fractures, severe burns, shrapnel wounds, and a leg amputation.

The La Penca bombing, as the event has become known, was blamed almost immediately on Sandinistas wanting to kill Pastora. But Tony Avirgan, who was wounded covering the event for ABC News, and his wife Martha Honey, another respected journalist, who was writing a breaking story for the *New York Times* on the day of the bombing and so stayed in San José, weren't so sure. They made a crusade of trying to find out what happened, partly simply as good investigative journalism, partly as a kind of therapy for Avirgan after such a horrible experience. Over a year later, after more than one hundred interviews, they reached some startling conclusions in a thirty-six-page report:

> Those responsible for the bombing include the Central Intelligence Agency, members of the MDN and FDN contra organizations, and Cuban-Amer-

icans in Miami. . . . The bombing was a right-wing
plot which was intended to be blamed on the Sandinistas. Its aim was first to kill Pastora. . . . Second,
it is likely the bombing was intended to increase ten-
sions between Costa Rica and Nicaragua. . . . Third,
by killing and maiming journalists, the bombing
would help turn the press and public opinion against
the Nicaraguan government.[16]

At a number of points in the report, John Hull is linked
to the CIA, to the contras, and even to a plot to kill Pastora.

To the naive and not so naive, the whole thing sounds
like the wildest kind of conspiracy theory. Yet both assassination and fabricating outrages against the United
States are unfortunate parts of our foreign policy. It is now
well documented that the CIA assassinated Salvador Al-
lende, the Marxist president of Chile, and tried many
times to kill Fidel Castro. It has also become clear with
time that the infamous Gulf of Tonkin provocation that
persuaded Congress to endorse the Vietnam War was an
event fabricated to whip up popular support. And from
Panama, more recently, have come disputed reports that
Oliver North was interested in creating a provocation
(much like La Penca could have been) as an excuse to invade Nicaragua.

But it's not precedent so much as evidence that makes
the Avirgan-Honey case compelling. Painstaking investigation leading from the Cuban-American community in
Miami back to the Costa Rican government, from mercenaries who had participated in the contra camps near Hull
to a close tracking of the man believed to have planted the
bomb, all pointed the journalists toward their conclusions.

Yet more work on the subject by CBS News Producer Leslie Cockburn not only backed up Honey and Avirgan, but went on to quote first-hand sources as saying that Hull, as the CIA's man, participated in drug smuggling as part of the contra arms-supply scheme.

In her book *Out of Control*, Cockburn quotes a pilot named Gary Betzner, who says, "I took two loads—small aircraft loads—of weapons to John Hull's ranch in Costa Rica and returned to Florida with approximately a thousand kilos of cocaine, five hundred each trip."[17] Betzner's boss in the operation, a Colombian-American named George Morales, told Cockburn that Hull received three hundred thousand dollars off the top of a drug-running trip as payment for using the strip. Independent of Cockburn's work, another drug-smuggling pilot reports that Hull's ranch was used as a loading point and that Hull definitely was aware of the activity.

What does Hull say about all these accusations? He says it is "bullshit" to conclude that the CIA tried to kill Pastora. Pastora had flown with Hull any number of times, he argues. "If I had wanted him dead, all I'd have to do is BANG, shoot him and push him out of my plane."

Hull believes that it was possible someone like Libya's Moammar Khadafy, whom he claims Pastora double-crossed, tried to kill the Nicaraguan. But even more plausible, says Hull, is that Pastora had the bomb planted himself, perhaps to generate sympathy and publicity. Pastora, Hull has decided, is still a Communist and still works for the Sandinista government.

As for the drug- and weapon-running? No way, insists Hull, maintaining that his effort was strictly "humanitarian." He has decided Honey and Avirgan are probably secretly subsidized Communist agents. In fact, Hull was so incensed about the allegations raised against him in regard to the La Penca bombing that he filed a libel suit against the journalists in Costa Rica. Unfortunately for Hull, the witnesses who were willing to appear at the trial and testify against him were formidable. They included Edén Pastora, a Miami public defender named John Mattes who had been tracking the flow of guns and drugs from Florida, a British mercenary named Peter Glibbery who said he had been on Hull's farm with contra fighters, and another mercenary named Jack Terrell who said he had attended a meeting with Hull and others after the La Penca bombing during which they talked about another plan to kill Pastora. The judge listened, considered, and dismissed Hull's libel suit as groundless.

Noticeably absent at the court was another mercenary named Steven Carr, who had disappeared the morning of the trial. Carr, like Glibbery, had been in jail in San José, following his arrest for weapons possession along the border, when he told Costa Rican journalists in 1985, "I'm pretty sure they're going to dust me off when I get back to the States. I pissed them off, ruined the FDN [contra] supply lines. I wish to God I'd never met a Cuban."[18] Carr apparently didn't want to get in any deeper than he was already, so didn't testify. But in the long run none of this mattered much for him: Before the end of 1986, he would be found dead in Panama City, California. According to Leslie Cockburn, three autopsies could not definitely pinpoint the cause of death, although a cocaine overdose was listed as a possibility. Whether it was self-inflicted remains unclear.

This international crowd that gathered around John Hull, replete with mercenaries, CIA operatives, underground Nicaraguans, perhaps even drug-smuggling South Americans and North Americans, was a far cry from the international crowd that has visited Wolf Guindon and Monteverde in recent years. Some of the world's best biologists, ornithologists, and entomologists have made the trek, attracted by the unique environment and all the life it sustains. The golden toad is only one of many fascinations: Scientists have studied the hummingbirds of the forest, the two-hundred-fifty-odd species of butterflies that migrate through, the way moss and trees interact and pass nutrients to each other. These people delight in the forest, climbing into the canopy of the trees to study the goings-on far above ground, turning over rotting stumps to look for salamanders, calling out with delight at various discoveries, rising with the sun to catch a glimpse of the elusive, colorful quetzal, Costa Rica's national bird.

The wet, emerald jewel of a forest has also begun to attract tourists, naturalists not as well trained as the scientists but still on the lookout for signs of a puma, a jaguar, a bare-necked umbrella bird, a monkey hooting through the trees. With the tourists come dollars, and small boarding houses have sprung up. Monteverde is on the map now and mentioned in all the guides, and sometimes the Quakers worry that notoriety is changing their community. There is even talk that the road up the mountain might be paved. The general feeling seems to be that change is inevitable and not necessarily bad, however, and if notoriety is the price to be paid for saving the cloud forest, then that is how it must be.

John Hull's notoriety, on the other hand, has resulted in quite a headache for him. The winds that began to blow the cover off his "dumb U.S. rancher" persona first kicked up when a plane flying weapons to the contras was shot down over Nicaragua late in 1986. Eugene Hasenfus, nothing but a "kicker," according to one source who flew numerous missions with him, nothing but the guy who loads and unloads the plane, lived to tell the tale. Hasenfus's story including using airstrips along northern Costa Rica, relying on protection from the United States government, and, he implied, becoming involved with officials who eventually reached all the way to the White House, the National Security Council, and the CIA. The Iran-contra scandal broke open, dragging information into the public domain that officially implicated Hull for the first time. None of it directly proved Tony Avirgan and Martha Honey's conclusions about the bombing at La Penca, but virtually all of it involved the same cast of characters and seemed to point in similar directions. A landmark lawsuit filed by the couple against what they see as an illegal organization responsible for the bombing (among many other things) is now working its way through federal appellate court in Miami, after a lower court judge issued a ruling dismissing the case. John Hull is among the defendants.

As a little fish in what has now become quite a big and murky pond, Hull seems to have been cut off by his old friends at the CIA, abandoned as a liability. "The bastards got me into this," he told *The Tico Times* in San José in July 1987. "The least they can do is protect my family. Now that I need . . . [financial support] most, they've cut it off due to the dog-and-pony show in Washington." Angry as that sounds, Hull didn't blame the CIA for the problems: "They had to choose people or use people like myself, who are untrained and inexperienced, because there was no way you could confide in Congress. And by now, surely to God, everybody in America knows you cannot trust anybody in Congress."[19]

By December 1987, sitting in his small office at home, Hull had become a bit more stoical about it all. "Abandoned?" he asks, echoing a question. "Hell yeah, but I don't mind. You know these things going in. See, the CIA was pretty well destroyed under Carter. And what Carter didn't, the press did."

Gone are the days when, according to one source, Hull and his midwestern compatriots would receive telephone messages to call a "Thomas" at the U.S. embassy in San José, at which time any one of three or four people would get on the line with instructions about where to fly, whom to meet, and what to do. These days, if you ask Bob Plotkin at the U.S. Embassy in San José about John Hull, he says, "He's in Washington most of the time now. You might catch him here, but mostly he's there." In fact, Hull is rarely if ever in Washington and has been in Costa Rica much more than Indiana.

The importance of all this runs far beyond his personal life, Hull feels. He believes himself to be on the battlefield. He believes that the game of dominoes we heard so much about in Southeast Asia is now being played in Central America. "If Costa Rica falls," he says, meaning to the Communists, "the ball game's over. Mexico can go in forty-eight hours, anytime the Communists want." And then all that's separating "them" from "us" is the Rio Grande.

And make no mistake, says Hull, diplomacy like the Arias peace plan may win Nobel Prizes, but it won't stop this scourge. "It's a dream," he says of such efforts. "I can remember when Neville Chamberlain, in 1939, came back from Germany waving a piece of paper, saying, 'Peace in our time.' Two years later, I was sitting in one of these Mosquitos [a fighter plane], not feeling too peaceful." Applying Hull's analogy, the Sandinistas become Nazis, Ortega is Hitler, and Costa Rica is some combination of Poland and Great Britain.

It all sounds somewhat absurd, but Hull was jettisoned from the CIA (at least publicly) not because of his views, but because of his exposure. And even these days his official contacts have not ended. For example, as he leafs through documentation that he planned to use in the trial against him in Miami, Hull pulls out "folio 12," which is a detailed computer printout of the movements of Martha Honey and Tony Avirgan, recording every time they have left Costa Rica, their destinations, and their time away. Friends in the Costa Rican government, he says, provided him with the material. This proves, he adds, that the couple must be receiving secret money, likely of Communist origin, to be traveling so extensively. (Actually, the records prove no such thing. They indicate a reasonable and logical amount of travel for a couple whose journalism has been commissioned by NBC, ABC, CNN, National Public Radio, the British Broadcasting Corporation, and the *New York Times*, among others. A more pressing question is how a private citizen like John Hull gets access to such government documents.)

According to Hull, among the benefits lost after he broke ties with the CIA is a "safe house" in San José, complete with bodyguards, for which he was receiving $1,100 a month. In the meantime investigators for the Justice Department and Congress have tried to figure out what happened to $374,000 in federally backed loans to a business Hull was supposed to set up to manufacture wooden handles. Did the money go to the contras? No, Hull told the *Boston Globe* in October 1987: "All of my activities were known and approved by Mr. Casey at the Central Intelligence Agency, Lieutenant Colonel North at the NSC, and the Costa Rican government. And what I did in these areas had nothing to do with my commercial enterprise." The factory just didn't work out, he said.

The Quakers' cheese factory, indeed the community of the Green Mountain, has worked out just fine. The board of directors of the business is now fully Costa Rican, and of the forty-four original settlers at Monteverde, nine remain. Some of their children have carried on, while others have left for the big cities of the world. Newcomers, often Quakers, have found their way, so that today Monteverde numbers around one hundred fifty residents, three times the original settlement.

And although they are not evangelical Quakers, although the Monteverdians made their journey to Costa Rica to escape political forces rather than try to change them, Quakers in Costa Rica have established the Friends Peace Center in San José. It is their idea of a "safe house," a place where people committed to nonviolence, to peace and justice, can gather. The Center sponsors speakers and organizes workshops that often address ways in which conflicts can be resolved without war. Members are involved in trying to improve conditions in the refugee camps of Central America. It is an idealistic sort of place, dismissed by hard-boiled people as so much liberal fluff. But just because it is gentle does not make its spirit weak. "That Peace Center could make a big impact," says Wolf Guindon, although he prefers to stay up in the clouds, among the dripping green.

The Quaker movement's impact already has been profound. These are people whose lives become examples, and in a small country such examples can go a long way. Their pursuit of peaceful coexistence has made them good neighbors and employers. Their sensitivity to the environment has made them good stewards of an endangered world, of tropical rain forests and golden toads and wilderness. Attracted by Costa Rica's best sense of itself, they have enhanced it. They have proven that not all Americans are ugly.

As for the web of intrigue and deceit around John Hull, its impact and legacy, there are fewer kind words to offer. If exposing efforts of his kind, and less than wholehearted support of the contras does indeed mean that the Communists will soon be knocking on the door of Texas, then this story will have the world's biggest ironic twist.

But if that doesn't happen, and if, as it now looks, the Arias government is able to stop the rush toward militarism and war that seemed about to break over northern Costa Rica, then the real ironic twist of the midwestern farmers might turn out to be this: Costa Rica has become a key shipment point for drug smuggling between South America and the United States. By May 1986, drug enforcement officials were reporting that 20 percent of the cocaine reaching the United States was passing through Costa Rica. And so a saying has cropped up around the country, embracing both the drug allegations and the "nine-to-five" nature of the "freedom fighters'" war. "The contras' hands are dirty," say the wags, "but their boots are clean."

Whether or not John Hull was personally involved in the early days of all this, it now seems clear that the clandestine movement of arms and men, secretly sanctioned by United States government officials, opened the door for the clandestine, wholesale movement of drugs. Once that door opens, it is very difficult to close. And the corruption that kind of open door policy represents has a way of sickening a culture. Journalist Martha Honey, still working in San José, summed it up best. "The legacy of the drug trafficking will remain long after the contras are gone," she predicted. "And that is very sad."

INTERMEDIO TRES (THIRD INTERLUDE)

The Big Dogs

It is Sunday and I am at La Cariari, the deluxe resort hotel on the outskirts of San José. There is golf, there is tennis, there is swimming, there is a casino, but La Cariari serves another function: This is where the big dogs like to stay, and this is where the big dogs like to cut their deals.

So it is not surprising to see, at poolside, a cluster of North American businessmen stretched out on chaise lounges. The focus is on three of them, arranged in a semicircle facing the pool and the sun.

In the middle is the oldest—call him Harold—a well-preserved, wealthy sixty-five on whom the good life shows in respectable ways: He has gray hair combed over his bald spot, health-club tan, yellow and orange bathing suit almost to his knees, face composed in the mask of business.

To his left is a classic gray fox—call him Max. He's a body-conscious fifty-four, with two gold chains glittering on his tanned, hairless chest, full white teeth, full head of gray hair, and blue bikini bathing suit—a James Coburn type. Max is joking with his young, mustachioed assistant who probably has a combined business and law degree and who sits in a straight-backed chair.

To Harold's right is a young turk nicknamed Bubba. Not yet forty, Bubba wears a big gold wristwatch that gleams when he runs his hands through blown-dry hair. Dark sunglasses are fastened to a string around his neck. He is no longer in shape and too young to wear a spare tire gracefully, the quietest of the three but focused, a combination of business bodyguard and street-smart dealmaker, who also has an assistant with him, carrying a clipboard.

Between this group and the pool, between this group and the sun, facing them all and unable to sit still is a big pear of a man who we'll call Donny. In his early forties, with a heavy gold and diamond ring on his right hand, Donny weighs 240 easily. His yellow bathing suit passes straight across the middle of his stomach, adding to the pear image. He is least tanned of them all, maybe because he seems constitutionally unable to remain in one position for more than a few seconds. To see this pear of a man become a bear of a man, gesturing, pacing, exuding even when he isn't talking (which is not often), is really rather extraordinary. His being is loud; even in silence he's on top of you, he's pushing. We are in the presence of a salesman.

153

"Look, here's what we'll do," Donny suddenly explodes, slapping his leg. "You put in twenty-five, I'll put in twenty-five, we all put in twenty-five. We get a Costa Rican corporation together to handle everything, all right? You realize how cheap this is? We're talking PROFIT. And NO taxes. DOLLARS." He pauses. No one says anything—no one even wants to look at him. "What? What do you think would happen? What? You wouldn't like two hundred grand coming in on the side, tax free? You think between canning and bottling we couldn't do it?"

He waits for an answer. There is no answer. No one is talking to him. Donny throws up his hands and takes a little walk around the pool, past the sunken bar where you can stay wet and get drunk. He's backing off, considering his next approach. With Donny out of the way a little small talk can spring up. Harold comments on the weather, how pleasant the dry, hot sun is. Max agrees, throwing his arms over his head, checking his tan. Bubba is whispering to his right-hand man, who makes a note on the clipboard.

"Yeah," calls Donny from the other side of the pool, working his way back. "You know why I like to come down here? Because January, February, March, you ALWAYS have good weather. ALWAYS. You go to Florida, you get rained on. Not here, baby, not here." He looks at their glasses. "Hey, you got something to drink? Waiter, a bottle of tequila. Max, I know you, you like tequila. That all right with you, Harold?"

"Jesus, Donny, it's a little early for that. Tell you what, I'll have some white wine."

"White wine it is. Waiter, a bottle of white wine. Bubba, what? Whatever you want, on me."

"Beer is good."

154

"And a cerveza, water, a cerveza. But promise me, you got to try this wonderful orange juice they got here. Did you try it yet? Isn't that wonderful? And have you tried the pineapple? Oh, PLEASE try the pineapples, you got to."

He's all the way back now. "Why can't we make pasta here? Huh? You know what they tell me? They say the fresh pasta isn't the best anyway." He looks around. Nothing. "Listen, if you can find a product, we can make that thing GO. This is the place for it, you understand? I mean, you like the concept, right?"

"I like the concept," says Harold, tired, quiet. "That's why I'm here. Why don't you relax, Donny. Sit, why don't you?"

"I can't, I'm just so excited and happy to be here, that's all." He begins to bounce up and down on the balls of his feet, his body jiggling, encouraged by the older man's politeness. "I'll tell you what we'll do. I'll sell—all right? I love it. I LOVE it. We'll set up a little office, I'll pay for it." He slaps his leg again. "And I'll SELL, don't worry. Hey, Harold, can we take a little walk for a second? Just around the pool. I got an idea, before I throw it out I want to talk about it, okay?"

Reluctantly Harold climbs to his feet, and they walk one lap around the pool. Max the gray fox tells Bubba the young turk a joke that involves "a broad and a traveling businessman." They laugh as Donny ushers Harold back to his lounge chair. "And we got a little guy," Donny is saying, "he's a mechanical and electrical engineer. We could send that little guy up to you and bring him right back. No problem." Harold sits, with a pained expression on his face.

"I really want to make rubber," Donny announces.

"That's really it. And I guarantee you, we go into molds
here, I can make it cheaper than anybody in the
WORLD. I GUARANTEE you. I got four machines just
sitting there, we could redo them and the whole bit. In
three years, we'll have fifty-five machines. Thirty-five million bucks. Christ, we'll be making so much money even I
won't be able to spend it. Everything's going to be auto-
mated and the property will be worth a fortune!"

Nobody jumps out of his chair, but for the first time
they're looking at him and looking at each other. Donny
senses a shift. "Max, take a walk with me," he implores.
"Just around the pool." Max takes his turn, strutting while
Donny works him, circles him, implores him. By the time
they make their lap Donny is saying, "So you guys want to
do a lawyer deal, is that it? Huh? A lawyer deal? Fine,
talk to the lawyers. Absolutely. But tell me this: You buy
the concept? You like the concept?"

"Easy does it, Donny," Max chuckles. "You're gonna
have a heart attack if you keep this up."

Donny stalks off, grimacing. "Christ, I bring you guys
down here, I do everything for you, and all he wants to do
is zing me."

"I'm not zinging you, I'm telling you the truth," says
Max.

Donny takes another lap, allowing the conversation to
turn social and get into the ins and outs of New York City
restaurants. "I'll tell you," says Donny, barreling back in.
"In New York, I like to have my five or six places where
they know me, and I always go, that's how I like to do it—
21, Primavera, they know me, they got a table for me, I
like that."

Everyone nods, nobody looks, Donny paces. Finally
Harold and Max butt heads for a while. Max's assistant has

stopped reading a *Sports Illustrated;* his gaze is fixed on the back of his boss's head. Bubba and his man huddle. Donny has just enough sense to know to lay off for a minute. When Harold motions for him to come back, he runs along the pool, all 240 pounds of him bouncing. Harold whispers in his ear.

"THAT'S the way, that's the WAY," Donny yells, bouncing up and down, so excited that his arms are moving too. He grabs Max and bearhugs him, kisses him on the lips, then lays a fat handshake on Harold. "Yeah, this is incredible! Waiter, more drinks for everybody. We need two pieces of equipment, that's it. YEAH. I LOVE IT."

Donny takes his fastest lap yet around the pool. Then he stops, seemingly stricken. The three of them have huddled again, a bad sign. "Hey, you got MY word on this now," he announces. "Please, please, don't back out on this. You got my word, I got your word. Bubba, come here, I want to talk to you." Bubba gets up for the ceremonial escort, but it is interrupted halfway around. "Hey," Donny yells, "you're not backing out of this! You cocksucker! No way, no WAY. It was fifty all the way around, plus another twenty-five. I had two hundred twenty-five, now I got one hundred seventy-five? No way, you're not backing out." A big parrot trapped in a cage under a thatched roof near the pool begins squawking, alarmed. The timbre of his call is remarkably similar to Donny's voice.

"Donny, you're too excitable," says Bubba, breaking away from him.

"Excitable? Yeah, I'm excitable. You can't take that away from me. I make deals. That's me."

Max has said a few words to his assistant, who jumps

157

out of his chair, intercepts Donny on the way back, and takes him to a neutral corner. They talk for about fifteen seconds. "Why, you cocksucker!" Donny explodes, running back to the big three. "Max, I don't even want to see him in my office, you understand?" Squawk, the parrot calls. Donny's blood pressure must be high enough to steam water.

"It's better people tell you now than later," says Harold, looking up at Donny towering over him.

"Sure, it's better you tell me now. Yes, it is. But, but . . ." He sputters, not knowing what to say, then resorts to the walking. One lap, two laps, three laps, finally he gets himself under control. "Waiter, give me a rum punch," he calls out. "You ought to taste these rum punches, PLEASE taste one of them. All right, what's the problem here? What can't we solve? Nothing, that's what." Donny's not giving up as easily as that, no sir, he didn't get these guys down to Costa Rica from New York to give up as easily as that. They just need to settle on the right product, that's all, and once they do there's no way they can't make money, the place is just begging you to come in and make money. They're not flying back until Monday morning; he's got a captive audience between now and then. They'll work something out, they'll work some business out . . .

In the evening, at the open-air bar, a guy who I'll call Tony really puts things into perspective. Tony is from Brooklyn, Tony is a very tough thirty-three years old, and Tony knows the fruit business. Tony also knows about jungle warfare, how to parachute into wild country and how to kill a man quickly. After a few beers, Tony might tell a few stories. Like on his first day of training, when his instructor walked up to him, nose to nose, stuck a cockroach in his hand, and ordered him to eat it. No problem, Tony gulped it. A few seconds later he began to feel something crawling up his insides. "Always remember," barked the instructor, plucking at his own cockroach before popping it down, "to take the legs off an insect before you eat it." Or like the time he had to kill a man using his knife in the jungle and he was so scared he might not do it right that he practically severed the guy's head right off his shoulders.

But those are different stories. These days, Tony knows from fruit and that's why he's in Costa Rica.

"This place is like Chile was ten years ago," he says. "It's still wide open, still a lot of land available to diversify the agriculture. And anything will grow." The climate is so great that, depending on what you want, all you got to do is go up or down the side of the mountains. Down below you get tropical, like bananas, cacao, or even pepper. Go up some and you get pineapples or oranges. Go up some more and you get strawberries or ornamental plants. As high as you want you get mountain coffee, good as Colombian. But Tony's not into coffee or palm oil. The return's too far down the line. He wants something you plant and you harvest, no waiting around for five years.

That's only the beginning of the advantages around here, Tony goes on in a heavy Brooklyn accent, boyish face over a barrel chest, hands that make a fist easily. Take strawberries. Strawberries don't like machines, they get all bruised up. Here in Costa Rica, it's low technology. People pick the fruit, just like the old days. That's great for strawberries, it's excellent. "Now all we need is a little rain, a little cold in California, and the Costa Rican planters will have a field day." And Tony, well, Tony is talking volume. If Tony makes a few cents on every carton of strawberries he moves, and if these Costa Ricans can understand the volume he's willing to handle, well, let's just say that a little number times a very big number makes for a very, very big number.

Meanwhile, a hectare—that's two and a half acres—can go for two thousand dollars around here—good growing land, says Tony, not dregs. Pay for one day of work here with the equivalent of one hour's wage back home and you don't even have anything on your conscience. Jesus, the people here live better than in the States on that. They got Social Security, everything. You want a good Costa Rican engineer? Pay him six thousand dollars, you got him.

"You know what else I like about this?" asks Tony. "I'm two hours from Miami. I'm in the same time zone as Chicago. I want to talk to a middleman here about setting up a dummy corporation, he speaks English. I want to talk about it with my partner in California, the phones work. These things I like, these things make it easy to make money."

And the government, the policy, you get major tax breaks for anything you export, you get free zone systems near the ports to move things easy, colones aren't traded on the international market and they're tied right to U.S. dollars so you're not likely to get caught in a wicked devaluation. And you're also not going to get caught in a military coup or a left-wing revolution. The government's stable. Sure there's a lot of paperwork and delay and bureaucracy, but not every single damned public servant has his hand out like in Mexico. As the saying goes, You can't buy a Costa Rican official—but you can rent one. Hey, that's more than can be said for New York City. You think the street vendor selling fruit on the same sidewalk of the

same block every day isn't paying some cop for the privilege? Sure, right. But you think he can't afford it? If he's
smart he's wearing his cutoff gloves and spelling the words
wrong on his cardboard signs on purpose—and making
more than most of the suit-and-tie execs buying his
Chilean grapes for a buck thirty a pound.

Anyway, see that guy over there? Tony points to a dark,
bald man in his mid forties, seated in a fantail wicker chair
on the other side of the bar and flanked by two young
Costa Rican beauties. Iranian, barely got his ass out before the revolution, came here along with a bunch of Iranians. Some of them were smart, some of them were
stupid. One guy took his 8 million bucks and decided that
coconuts were the thing, so he bought up a huge tract of
land, built some housing for workers, and had them plant
coconut trees. Didn't ask around, didn't take his time, figured he knew everything, didn't bother to find out about
the disease that had wiped out coconuts in the area, which
is why there seemed to be such a big opening for them. A
few years later he had to sell everything for $500,000. The
smart ones, like this guy with the women, they start small
and build up, they get to know what's happening and
who's happening; if they make a mistake they lose small, if
they were right, well, then all it means is the return
shows up six months or a year later.

"WHISKEY," yells a big Texan of a golfer, seated on
the other side of Tony, slamming his glass down on the
mahogany bar, stopping conversations. A Costa Rican
waiter comes rushing over. "That's how you do thangs
'round heeyah," he drawls to his buddy.

Tony and I look at each other, more or less embarrassed
to be near such a display. Funny thing is, whether it's
politics or business, foreign policy or import-export, the

Texan's not far from right. It *is* how gringos do things down here and have been doing things for a long time—which makes Oscar Arias's job that much more difficult and his achievements that much more impressive.

I'd be seeing the president in the morning, so I needed to get some sleep. On the way through the lobby I heard an unmistakable sound. No, it was not the parrot squawking. It was Donny, bringing his associates back from a San José dinner for a couple of nightcaps. He was smoking a cigar, he was smiling, and of course he was talking. Only one thing could make him feel that good: They'd cut a deal.

CHAPTER SEVEN

The Making of a President

Costa Rica's Presidential House sits in a nondescript industrial district about ten minutes from downtown. The street is just wide enough to let two cars pass. Across the street is an empty lot full of weeds, enclosed by a barbed wire fence knocked together with two-by-threes. Next door is Industrious Langer SA, a manufacturing operation. On the other side is Pulperia y Cantina Villa Nueva, a little quickstop for cigarettes and milk, with a green corrugated roof, blue trim, and beige walls. Soda La Burbuja, a fast food joint, is beside Langer and below, Cocinas Venta Cambio Reparación, a kitchen appliance sales and repair outlet. Banco Nacional de Costa Rica is catty-corner, be-

163

side Floristeria Anna, a flower shop. A soccer game on a makeshift field picks up occasionally across the street.

A wall about ten feet high circles Casa Presidencial. It is not very imposing, and the effect is further softened by a hibiscus hedge that runs up five feet and spatters bright red flowers in pointillist fashion. A tall gate blocks the entrance driveway. People gather in front, at a small booth where guards sit and examine credentials, and tell the guards why they have come, who they are looking for. If these people really wanted to, they could open the gate themselves simply by reaching in and turning the latch. But the guards open and close the gate, telephone people inside, open briefcases to check for weapons, and wave people along. A woman has come for a cleaning job interview. A priest has come to see about a cultural program. A journalist has come to interview the president.

The building is less than a stone's throw from the street. In the small front yard there is a shallow, stagnant pool rimmed with bushes and grass. Two of the mysterious basalt balls of Costa Rican antiquity stand guard, flanking the front door, one perfectly smooth and one carved. The facade of the building is low and long, concrete and plate glass. There is nothing ornate about it, nothing symbolic of power and glory. It has a very businesslike, pragmatic aura. There are no labyrinthine halls where one can wander with jaw agape at the majesty and complexity of the seat of government. There are no marble columns that dwarf the visitor. At the front door there is a secretary, not a security officer or walkie-talkied Secret Service agent, and the secretary buzzes you in. In short, the place is very Costa Rican in its lack of pretension. After the pomp and circumstance of our White

House, or the opulence protected by machine guns at the presidential house in Haiti, this is a welcome change.

It is hard to make a renovated fertilizer factory pretentious, and that's exactly what this building was. The local joke is that only the form of fertilizer has changed, but the real point is that people can say as much any time they want without having to worry that they will "disappear" soon after.

Inside the building there is a large rectangular pool with fountains around a courtyard. Ferns and other plants soften the marble floors and concrete walls. Various office doors open onto the courtyard. On the upper left is the office of the president.

Costa Rican presidents have two rooms in which they meet people and conduct interviews. Both are elegant but understated. The inner room resembles a den, with the president's desk, a television set hooked up to U.S. stations via satellite, a glass-topped coffee table in front of a sofa, and a few comfortable chairs. A beige rug and beige curtains counterpoint a dark green wall, trimmed with gold. The outer room is more formal, more a room for entertaining, but it has the same dark green and beige motif. Watercolors of classic tico naturalism adorn the walls. There are many pictures of the president's family, his wife Margarita and his two children Sylvia and Oscar Felipe. There is also a bust of Arias. "The president prefers to be photographed from the left side," whispers a press aide, the side with a small beauty mark on his cheek.

So vanity does play a part in Oscar Arias Sánchez's life. His suits are carefully cut, elegantly conservative. He almost always wears a tie in public; his hair invariably is in place. His physical presence shows an attention to detail but no flamboyance; it is strictly masculine. Don Pepe can wear Mao jackets, but Arias prefers pleated trousers and bulky U.S. sweaters when he's at home.

To see Arias in the presidential offices *is* to see a man at home. Clearly his entire life has been directed toward this end, and he has not been bashful about saying so. On the campaign trail, in 1985, he announced, "Since I was in my mother's womb, I prepared myself for this. Even if I wanted to lose, it wouldn't be possible." As far back as 1967, in a yearbook of the University of Costa Rica, he wrote, "I am studying to be President."[20]

His certainty has been seen as a form of megalomania, or at least egomania, and yet the person who sits at the president's desk has neither of those qualities. The adjectives that come to mind are ambitious, stubborn, single-minded, willful, logical, pragmatic, patient, and principled in a way no maniac could be. And so his certainty and his success make you wonder more about destiny, and the calling of history, than about his psychological makeup.

He was born September 13, 1941, near the town of Heredia in Costa Rica's Central Plateau. Both the Arias and Sánchez families were part of Costa Rica's young coffee aristocracy, among the richest families of the country. Yet when Arias refers to his roots he prefers to mention his grandfather, a humble ox-cart driver who worked hard and slowly began to amass money, then land, and then more land. As is so often the case with hardworking, successful people, higher education for the next generation was a priority that ranked with consolidating and strengthening the coffee business.

Two generations later, the family fortune had become something that needed to be managed, not made. So, continuing the classic pattern, the third generation sought success in the intellectual world and the public arena of politics. That was where the social responsibilities and privileges of wealth could be balanced and that was where the ambitious next generation could find opportunity to leave its own indelible achievements. Perhaps all this, more than historical destiny, explains Oscar Arias's certainty about his public career.

This is not to say that politics did not enter the Arias and Sánchez families before Oscar's arrival. Arias's father had run unsuccessfully as a vice-presidential candidate in the 1970s with Luis Alberto Monge, who would eventually win the presidency in the term before Arias's. The family was Liberación, in agreement with Figueres and opposed to Calderón. Figueres would have a deep and lasting effect on Arias's political thinking, as he would on so many of Arias's generation.

And Arias clearly was a thinker. The eldest of three, he was plagued by asthma in his youth, making physical activity difficult and sleep sometimes elusive. As a result, Arias would stay up late, reading voraciously and widely, absorbing, considering, studying. Such experiences can be lonely; they do not incline children toward light-hearted personalities. But they do encourage depth, perseverance, and a life of the mind.

After a high school experience structured on strong Roman Catholic principles, Arias did what many wealthier Costa Ricans do: He left the country for more schooling and to broaden his horizons. Like Figueres before him, Arias chose Boston. But unlike Figueres, more like Calderón, Arias decided he wanted to become a doctor. Although there has been a widespread misconception in Costa Rica that Arias attended Harvard Medical School,

THE MAKING OF A PRESIDENT

actually he enrolled at Boston University as an under-
graduate pre-med student. The year was 1959. He lived
in a dorm called Myles Standish in the Kenmore Square
section of Boston, which was a hub of student activity
even in those days.

"I like Boston so very much," says Arias. "I still miss
it." It was his first time living abroad, and Boston seemed
to represent a coming-out for him. He became a fan of
Boston's Symphony Hall, attending concerts conducted by
Charles Munsch and following the players out to Tan-
glewood for summer concerts. "All the money I could
save was for music, theater, and opera," he remembers.

He sometimes went to the more bohemian side of the
Charles River, to Harvard Square in Cambridge. "I remember going into a bar, I guess you'd call it, where a
singer who knew Spanish used to sing. She was quite unknown at the time, 1959, and all I knew about her was she
knew Spanish, so I could talk Spanish with her." The
singer was Joan Baez, and the bar was the famous Club
47, where Bob Dylan played to crowds of maybe fifty people and the strongest drink available was espresso. To this
day, Arias's musical taste ranges from opera to some of
Latin America's newest protest songs.

As for academics, Arias was finding that the pre-med
subjects of botany, zoology, and chemistry almost immediately took a back seat to social science courses, such as
sociology, anthropology, and history. "I found out I was in
the wrong field," he says, chuckling. "I was too smart to
be a doctor." A few months at Harvard summer school
between semesters only reinforced those feelings, intro-
ducing Arias to the thinking of economist John Kenneth
Galbraith, whom he had not yet been exposed to. "All of

this really opened my mind," he says, "and had a tremendous impact on my future."

But most important of all, Arias was in Boston while John Kennedy was running for president against Richard Nixon. "I saw the campaign," he remembers. "I saw the debates. This had a tremendous impact on me." Indeed, Arias seemed to absorb the JFK experience and internalize it in a deep, personal way. It would become increasingly clear as he pursued his public career that the Kennedy mystique and style were an inspiration that went beyond the kind of mimicry that Gary Hart or Senator John Kerry from Massachusetts have practiced. Arias fit into Costa Rican society the way Kennedy fit into North American society: He too was a liberal from a wealthy, politically ambitious, self-made family. Beyond stylistic similarities, beyond rumors of womanizing, beyond even appointing his younger brother Rodrigo to a key government post much as JFK appointed Robert, Arias would come to represent a new political order. "The torch must be passed to a new generation," Arias would proclaim during his presidential campaign, twenty-five years after he first heard those words in Boston.

Actually, according to Arias, the president-elect and the college student president-to-be had some personal contact. "I remember writing a long letter to President Kennedy once he was elected," Arias recalls, "later published in the Boston University paper. It was called, 'This Is How I See It,' and it was about Central America and what Central Americans expected from the new administration." The letter talked about the failures of Eisenhower; how his neglect and shortsightedness contributed to the rise of Castro. Unfortunately, no one at Boston University or the Kennedy Library can locate a copy of the letter, but Arias must have been eloquent. "After that," he recalls, "I got an invitation to go to Hyannisport to visit him." Again, there is no documentation of the visit, but Arias remembers it as short and cordial—and the sort of thing you mention for the rest of your life.

In a way, the entirety of Arias's Boston experience is summed up by that description. Less than two years into college he conclusively came to terms with the fact that medicine was not his calling. He returned to Costa Rica, minus a degree but with much experience under his belt, and entered the University of Costa Rica in San José to study law and economics. Arias graduated in 1967, but the urge to study abroad was still strong, so this time he left for England with a scholarship from the British government, where from 1967 until 1969 he pursued a masters in political science from the University of Essex and the London School of Economics.

The British part of Arias's years abroad seemed to offer a more sober inspiration. He was older, after all, less wide-eyed, and a seminal personality like JFK rarely surfaces to influence a life. Rather, Arias absorbed more of a cultural influence. He respected the civility, the calm reason of the British (even as their members of Parliament screamed at each other during debate). He came to value negotiation, compromise, pragmatism—some of the British calling cards of diplomacy. The British emphasis on these traits allows them to look at the United States as a kind of aggressive, muscle-bound, self-centered adolescent. Arias seemed to come to terms with this, although his thesis and study centered on Costa Rica's political system. In the years ahead, he would not forget to involve Europe in his diplomacy, to work international opinion as a counterweight to United States domination of his region.

By 1969 Arias had returned to Costa Rica and become a professor of political science at the University. He was also writing what would become his first book, originally published as a national prizewinning essay. *Grupos de Presión en Costa Rica* (Pressure Groups in Costa Rica), was no earth-shattering social manifesto but an interesting, closely reasoned analysis of a small democracy in action. At the heart of the argument was Arias's belief that groups rather than individuals exert the forces that move governments. There is nothing wrong with that idea—indeed, there is a lot to be said in favor of such organized access to power—but it means that government itself must be strong enough to maintain a certain equilibrium and to keep in mind the greater common good, which none of these pressure groups cares to see. Without the rudder and ballast of a central government, not only does the direction of policy zigzag but the people who do not have access to these pressure groups are pitched overboard.

It was a sense of government in line both with the legacy of FDR's New Deal Democratic Party and Great Britain's Labour Party, with its working-class roots. And, therefore, it was clearly in line with Costa Rica's Liberación Party in general and with the philosophy of José Figueres in particular. Arias must have known this; he dedicated his early political writing to Figueres, among others.

The rewards were not long in coming. Figueres saw Arias as one of the party's young hopefuls, a rising star of the coming generation. When Figueres resumed the presidency in 1970, he appointed Arias to the largely ceremonial post of economic adviser to the president. Then, in

August 1972, Figueres upped the ante and named Arias to the equivalent of a cabinet-level position as minister of national planning. Arias was thirty-one years old.

The post was not one of the higher-profile slots in the government, but it put Arias on the inside and gave him legitimacy. It also gave him good reason to tour the country, meeting people, understanding economic dynamics, and making political contacts. For example, a young Costa Rican named Otton Solis remembers when he first met Arias, in 1976, toward the end of Arias's tenure as minister of planning. Arias had come to the southern part of the country, near San Isidro, where Solis was serving on a local council of cooperatives and public planners. Solis was only twenty-one years old but he was pragmatic and smart enough to realize that he should be specific and direct and not ask for the moon from the minister. "Over lunch, with all the politicians, we talked," Solis remembers. "From there we were going to see a sugar mill, and Oscar said, 'Can I drive with you?' Of course. And on the way I only asked for two things: better rural roads, and a technical agricultural school. After that, we became friends."

Ten years later, as Arias was forming his own government, he would call Solis, then in England, and ask him if he wanted to come home and become for Arias what Arias had been for Figueres: minister of planning and economic policy. Within two days, Solis was ensconced in the government.

It was also during this time, 1973, that Arias married. Margarita Penón Gongora was, like Arias, wealthy. Her family's money came from a successful furniture business begun two generations earlier. She also had gone to the United States for schooling, graduating from Vassar as a

biochemistry major before returning to Costa Rica. In the
JFK analogy, she certainly has drawn comparisons to Jac-
quelyn Kennedy for her sense of culture and her looks.
Yet she seems more intellectually accomplished, relies on
substance more than style, and probably has more influence on and a better relationship with her husband. She is
also more seriously involved in politics, particularly the
party politics of Liberación.

Arias would not have a glorious path to the presidency,
like Figueres. He would work his way up, paying his dues
rung by rung. He was not an electrifying speaker, he was
not blustery, he was not innately comfortable in crowds
and within the carnival of politics. In many ways he remained a shy, quiet reader, best one on one. He would
become known as an uncharismatic man. Yet he was respected for the Ph.D. he received in 1974 from the University of Essex and accorded the distinguished title of
Doctor. He wrote thoughtful books—his next ¿Quién
Gobierna en Costa Rica? (Who Governs in Costa Rica?)
appeared in 1976. He was appointed the Liberación
Party's international secretary in 1975. And he was elected a deputy to the legislature from Heredia in 1978
(equivalent to a congressman). Even so, as a legislator,
just as when he was a minister, his career showed no fire-
works. Where was the spark?

Even when Arias decided to run for secretary general of
the party in 1979, a clear sign that he was positioning himself for an eventual move toward the presidency, there
was no thunder, no lightning. "He really started working
the party at this point," says Eduardo Ulibarri, editor in
chief of La Nación, Costa Rica's biggest and most influential newspaper and a publication that has strongly opposed

Figueres, Arias, and Liberación over the years. "He was very quiet, but very strong, ambitious, and constant."

By July 1979, Arias surprised the party regulars by winning the secretary general post. People were beginning to understand that there was staying power to the man, that there was muscle even if there wasn't a whole lot of glitter. In 1983, when Arias was reelected as secretary general, there was less surprise that he had won and more recognition that he was a force to be reckoned with.

Just a year earlier, in 1982, Luis Monge, from Liberación, a longtime compatriot of Figueres, had won the presidency. Monge has been something of a Ronald Reagan figure in Costa Rica, one of the "Generation of 1948," who was accepted and even loved by a large segment of the population although he seemed out of touch with details, often misguided in policy, and had allowed corruption into his government. To complete the analogy, the man Monge replaced, Rodrigo Carazo, had been much like Jimmy Carter: relatively young and idealistic yet wrapped up in detail and regarded by the public as a failure of a president.

It seems in retrospect that from the beginning of the Monge presidency Arias knew that he would run next. And perhaps that ambition more than anything else alienated him from the older members of the party. Monge didn't particularly like him. Daniel Oduber, a former president and close friend of Figueres, didn't want Arias to be the party nominee. And, most of all, Figueres didn't want Arias to run in 1986.

Figueres had other plans. He saw himself making one last triumphant swing through the country and serving one last triumphant term as president. There were private meetings at which Figueres told everyone of his ambition.

He would say that Arias was still too young, that 1990 would be Arias's year. Figueres pictured himself and Oduber running together and called the ticket "the magic formula."

Taking nothing away from Don Pepe, it seems clear that his running would have been a mistake, for his own legacy more than anything. Campaign rhetoric aside, the time had come for a new generation of political leadership to establish some continuity with the 1948 crew and to bring a fresh perspective to the complexities of Costa Rican society. What's more, Don Pepe's day was probably over: Costa Rica is a young country; most of the voters had been born since the famous exploits of 1948. Seventy percent of its 1.4 million voters are less than forty years old; 500,000 are between eighteen and twenty-four. Figueres was revered or reviled by turns, but to all he represented the past, not the future.

Call it stubbornness, call it guts, but only Arias stood up to Don Pepe and refused to step aside for the 1986 campaign. Figueres would not participate without unanimous backing, and Arias had built enough bridges as secretary general to hold his own. Angry, perhaps bitter, Figueres supported Carlos Manuel Castillo against Arias in the primary that would decide the 1986 Liberación candidate.

"It was very tough for me to become a candidate," Arias says. "It was a very tough internal campaign." Both for psychological and political reasons, Arias didn't want to alienate Figueres, who was a national (and perhaps personal) father figure. But he felt that the generational split was symbolic of real differences. The older party members, who backed Castillo, referred to Arias's supporters as "young Turks," or even more derisively as "the mini-

skirts." Arias did not back down from this, as Eduardo U-
libarri, editor of *La Nación*, remembers: "Rather than
underplay this split, with its generational component,
Arias thought it was good for him to present it as a show of
personal force."

Perhaps this wasn't charisma, but it was backbone. And
Arias had one more crucial factor playing in his favor: For
the first time, the primary was going to be opened up to
any voter enrolled in the party, rather than a convention-
style decision of party regulars. It was a reform within
Liberación, an attempt to bring decision-making out of
the Costa Rican equivalent of the smoke-filled room, and
it dovetailed perfectly with the Arias campaign themes.
Arias appealed directly to younger voters—more liberal
urban constituents who might be called the tico version of
yuppies. He was sophisticated in his social techniques,
reaching beyond the party apparatus. And on February 1,
1985, a year before the general election, seven hundred
Liberación polling centers around the country recorded
about 250,000 votes, 10 percent of the population. Arias
beat Castillo by a comfortable 150,000 to 100,000.

"It was a dramatic success," remembers Ulibarri. "Almost better than the general election." But the bitterness
of the fight took its toll within Liberación. The older generation paid lip service to Arias but held back from real
support. Not only was Arias only forty-four years old (the
exact age at which John Kennedy ran for president), but
he surrounded himself with equally young or even younger men as his closest advisers. The warhorses resented
this. He also moved outside the party apparatus for support and counsel. John Biehl, a brilliant Chilean-born personal friend, wrote speeches and provided ideas. Guido
Fernandez, who had been editor of the dreaded opposi-

tion newspaper *La Nación* for twelve years, announced his support for Arias two weeks after the primary. For the general public, a defection like Fernandez's carried weight and helped broaden the campaign's base. But for the party regulars, it meant a lessening of their influence. And finally, in the flip-flop of Costa Rican elections, this seemed destined to be the year of anti-Liberación because in 1982 Monge had been elected.

And so who was the opposition candidate, the hands-on favorite to become the forty-eighth president of Costa Rica? None other than Rafael Angel Calderón, also known as "Junior," the son of the infamous Calderón of the 1940s who had been Figueres's arch enemy, the son of the man who had tried to annul the 1948 elections to stay in power, the son of the man who had openly or tacitly supported several invasions of Costa Rica from Nicaragua— the son of the man who still had a devoted group of supporters within the country, a bedrock 25 to 30 percent of the voters.

Only a Costa Rican could really understand how such an extraordinary turn of events could come to pass, how a legacy that included outrageous attempts to undermine democracy was not a kiss of death for the family name in that democracy. Partly it was because people loved the older Calderón in spite of it all. As a physician and president he seemed passionate in caring about poor people. And, partly, it was because people were impressed by Junior's own strengths as a politician.

Calderón Junior was born while his father was in exile in Nicaragua and spent his early years in Mexico, where he learned Spanish with the Mexican sing-song accent that Costa Ricans tend to make fun of. Four years younger than Arias, he possesses many qualities as a politician that

Arias lacked: He is charming, at ease in crowds, a dramatic speaker, charismatic on the stump, attractive. He had had government experience in the last anti-Liberación Carazo regime. He clearly had the strong backing of Costa Rica's most influential newspapers. Calderón even managed a visit with the bigwigs in Washington, where such men as George Bush and George Schultz all but endorsed him for the presidency. He had run for the presidency once before and had lost to Monge, which fit the pattern of candidacies that were successful the second time around. Every indicator seemed to be pointing toward Calderón; every pundit proclaimed that 1986 was his year.

This sense of an inevitable swing between Liberación and anti-Liberación suggests that perhaps Costa Rica's democracy is more a game played among a small group of insiders than a real bare-knuckled egalitarian brawl, a civilized seesaw with everyone accepting the rules of the sport. Certainly Arias was no outsider, no maverick. At first glance, the cut of his cloth was not so dramatically different from Calderón's. Just as cynics in the United States say that there is no difference between Democrats and Republicans, Costa Rican cynics dismissed Arias and Calderón as flip sides of the same coin.

They would be proven wrong. Nuances of style and content separated them from the start, and as the campaign built in intensity, those nuances gradually became major rifts. This would become an election of real substance and real alternatives.

As Calderón began to develop his campaign, several key themes emerged. First, as he would say, "I am not neutral and I am definitely on the side of the United States." With Green Berets and an increasing amount of

military hardware and training showing up on the northern border, Calderón did not seem passionate about de-
fending Costa Rica's pacifism. On the contrary, he was
willing to consider a further escalation of the role of the
Rural Guard, which seemed headed toward becoming an
army in everything but name. Back in 1979, Costa Ricans
had cheered in the streets when the Sandinistas won, but
public opinion had shifted radically against them. Just
about the only person in Costa Rica who had anything
good to say in public about the Sandinistas was Don Pepe.
Calderón was as anti-Sandinista as they came.

Calderón also played up the Reaganesque crowd-pleaser
theme that government is more a part of the problem than
the solution. He talked about socialist white elephants, how
the government loses money trying to behave like the private sector, how the size of government should be reduced,
how the bureaucracy should become more efficient, how
free enterprise could be freer. The active, intervening,
balancing force of government Arias espoused in his first
book was not a part of Junior's outlook. Neither did Junior
sound much like his father, who pushed hard for government programs like Social Security and better health care.

Costa Rican campaigns do not drag on interminably, as
they do in the United States. Yet even so, Arias was slow
getting out of the blocks. His restrained style, his lack of
hoopla were not well suited to the role of an underdog
looking for attention. He emphasized his training, his education, his wide range of interests, all of which qualified
him for the office. He positioned Calderón as a typical glib
politician capitalizing on his father's name. He resurrected
the original motto of Liberación, "Growth with Justice,"
as his campaign theme. He reminded the public that it
was easy to say that government is the problem, but in a

country where one in five people works for the government, where government jobs are the most common form of welfare, the argument rings hollow. "We had a choice between a welfare state and a garrison state," Arias would say, as quoted in *The Tico Times,* "and we chose the former. But it does have its disadvantages."[21]

And Arias also began to enunciate themes, both symbolic and concrete. He chose as one of his vice-presidential running mates (there are two in the Costa Rican system) Professor Victoria Garron, the first woman to run for vice-president, and he promised that women would have better jobs and access in his administration. In domestic politics he hammered away at two themes: housing and jobs. An Arias government, he promised, would create twenty thousand housing units a year for four years, and twenty-five thousand new jobs a year for four years. He called on his years as minister of planning in promising to work to strengthen cooperatives and improve exports.

Finally, he emphasized the idea that his personal integrity was above repute. The general notion seemed to be that, first, he was too rich to be tempted toward corruption and, second, he was too principled to allow such immorality. The Arias campaign song, which began to waft its way across the airwaves, included the lyrics, "A sincere heart, an intelligent mind, a firm and certain hand."

But his campaign style, at least among those who thought they understood such things, continued to weigh him down. One observer remembers a television commercial in which Arias did nothing more than sit at his desk, look straight into the camera, and in a low-key way tell people six things that he intended to do as president. Arias released a 155-page report, "The People's Mandate for Building the Future." It had plenty of ideas, it was in fact an excellent blueprint, but it was not the stuff of high emotion. His campaign became a joke among the well-heeled North American community that would disparage his seriousness, his bushy eyebrows, and his jowly face. Calderón was more flamboyant and more fun. And Calderón, they all insisted over cocktails, would win.

The polls were saying the same thing. So Arias, with that combination of pragmatism and vision that is becoming his trademark, huddled with his advisers in October and emerged with a new, stronger direction to the campaign. Arias would become the *peace* candidate. He would speak yet more directly to Costa Rica's national identity as a country without an army. He would attack Calderón's militarist instincts.

In retrospect it was the perfect approach. It was good politics because it read the public sentiment well, and it released something in Arias: It allowed him to become a better campaigner because he obviously believed deeply in what he was saying. By early November none other than Don Pepe Figueres announced that he was resigning his position as roving ambassador to campaign for Arias. "As long as there's a Calderón looking to be elected," Figueres proclaimed, "he'll find me ready to oppose him." Not exactly a ringing endorsement of Arias, but good enough.

Still there was a delicate balance Arias had to strike in this campaign for peace. He didn't want to be misunderstood as opposed to the United States, yet he wanted to proclaim neutrality. He would refer to Costa Rica's strong democratic tradition as a "vaccine" that would protect the country from the instability and violence of Central America, but at the same time he would insist that neutrality was the only way to avoid getting drawn into the war and bloodshed of Nicaragua to the north. He would speak of the close bonds between Costa Rica and the United States, how those ties must be kept strong, but he would appeal to the form of nationalism that believed Costa Rica shouldn't be at the beck and call of the superpower, that it could forge its own policy. He would comment on the fondness Costa Ricans feel when they think back on the help the United States offered in 1955, when an invasion from Nicaragua threatened the Figueres government—and if a history buff happened to recall that a Calderón was behind the scenes of that invasion, so much the better.

The new emphasis began to bring results. Although the campaign continued to be referred to as among the quietest in memory, by early December Arias pulled ahead in public opinion polls for the first time. Both candidates charged hard through the first two weeks of December, Arias alone holding almost two dozen rallies. And then, with Costa Rican priorities properly in place, a political truce was called; no propaganda was allowed from December 15 through January 3 to give everyone the time to enjoy Christmas and the New Year.

The campaign resumed with a month to go until the election, and in that month the tone got progressively meaner. Calderón began harping on what he said were connections between the Liberación Party and Communists in general, not to mention the Sandinistas in particular. A political ad showed a man wearing a hat of the organization COPAN and a T-shirt endorsing Arias. (COPAN, a group interested in providing housing for working people, is reputed to have a Trotskyite philosophy.) "COPAN is a Communist organization," read the copy of the ad. "COPAN supports Oscar Arias. What commitments will Arias make to get Communist support?"

The historical irony was phenomenal: Calderón's father had cut a deal with the Communist Party to remain in power.

Calderón also took to attacking his opponent personally. Under a smiling picture of Arias appeared the caption, "Only he who has a lot can laugh at the high cost of living." Two pictures of Arias side by side, looking in opposite directions, were captioned, "You can't trust a man who won't look you in the eye." Calderón ridiculed Arias's call for twenty thousand new housing units a year, saying that to fulfill the promise would mean building twelve houses every working hour. *"Adelante Costa Rica"* had been Calderón's early slogan, Forward Costa Rica. But in a mark of some campaign confusion, it was changed to say, *"Adelante Calderón por el Bien de Costa Rica,"* Forward Calderón for the Good of Costa Rica.

The Arias campaign stuck with *"El Camino de Futuro,"* The Road to the Future. "Vocation, Will and Commitment," an Arias campaign slogan announced. "A man who always says and does what he thinks." But Liberación was not above character smears either. Below a particularly poor photo of Calderón appeared the question, "Would you trust this man?" As February approached, the two sides took turns calling each other charlatans, liars, and worse.

By the way, such extensive advertising and campaigning is supported by public money, another extraordinary sign of Costa Rica's commitment to democracy and equal access. The law basically provides for 2 percent of the national budget to be earmarked for campaign expenses, meaning roughly $5 million, or two dollars for every Costa Rican. The money is divided among the major parties according to the percentage of vote they got the last time around, so the party in power has a slight financial advantage.

But such a small disparity would not hold back Cal-derón. Calderón on the stump was Calderón in his ele-ment. "He was like an electoral machine," said one journalist who covered the campaign. "His purpose was to win votes, and this was something he had spent all of his life doing, literally since adolescence, going after votes. No one taught him how to speak. It is simply something he does very well."

Arias, meanwhile, did not have the style to appeal to emotions. He appealed to ideas. But when the idea was the most emotional one of all, peace, the style seemed to work. Dogged, focused, Arias refused to let go of it. And peaceful neutrality played particularly well to the very groups he was courting—the young, the urban middle class, and women. Traditionally, Liberación's strength has tended toward the countryside, the landed middle class that makes up a great deal of Costa Rica's population. But Arias was striking into the new professional class of San José, which had a double interest in turning his way: All of Calderón's talk about scaling back government led many of them to wonder whether *their* jobs could be lost in the new efficiency.

With all of the calm conclusiveness of hindsight, the pieces of the picture were coming together. But the soothsayers were picking Calderón right through January. "I never thought Arias would win the election, right up until the last fifteen days," said *La Nación*'s Ulibarri, al-though some of that might have been wishful thinking—the paper's positions are far to the right of Arias. Yet Ulibarri was not alone; although opinion polls were in-conclusive, Arias remained the underdog in the public mind.

And then, finally, came February 2, 1986.

Election Day Costa Rica style is like nothing we know in this country. Part Mardi Gras (though the bars are closed), part July 4th, the enthusiasm of the day is its best characteristic save one; the scrupulous honesty of the vote. "Richard Daley would never have made it here," former U.S. Ambassador Lewis Tambs was quote as saying after his first Costa Rican election day.[22]

But of course the clean count makes for the lack of cynicism. Most Costa Ricans cannot understand the apathy that attends United States elections—the low voter turnout and lack of celebration. They do not take their democracy for granted, and this day proves it.

The polls opened February 2, 1986, at 5 AM, and already it seemed as though the country was draped in bunting. Tradition dictates that people hang the flag of the party they support, either red and blue for Calderón or green and white for Arias. Sometimes family disagreements would surface for all to see: A house might bristle with two green and white flags and one red and blue. "My mother thinks Figueres is a Communist, and my father thinks Figueres is a democrat," explained one man in his twenties. "Me, I voted for Arias."

Absentee ballots do not exist, so the day also became one for reunions and travel. Traffic jams inevitably turned parts of San José into parking lots, as drivers took advantage of the delays to shout slogans and engage in last-minute politicking: Two honks were for Os-car, while three blasts announced a Cal-de-rón backer. Arguments might occasionally break out, but violence was unheard of.

Staying away from the polls, either as a protest or from laziness, is also extremely rare. Back in 1959, after Liberación lost a close election, the government declared that voting was mandatory. There are no enforced penalties for not voting, but Costa Ricans must register to get the equivalent of a domestic passport that helps cut red tape for health care and other public services. People vote for positive reasons, civic pride and involvement, more than because they fear any repercussions if they don't. On February 2, of 1.4 million eligible voters, nearly 1.2 million, roughly 85 percent, made their way to the polls.

When they got there they were handed three ballots, one for President, one for Congress, and one for municipal positions. The presidential ballot, for example, included the name, photograph, and party colors of each candidate as crosschecks—just to make sure no one was confused. In the time-honored tradition of Costa Rican elections, voters stuck their thumbs into purple ink and then pressed their thumbprints into the box of the candidates they wanted to win. The ballots were then folded and poll watchers made sure that they were deposited in the ballot boxes without shenanigans. After voting people reached for napkins to wipe off the ink, and when napkins ran out the walls of some voting places were dotted with purple thumbmarks. But the ink will not come off completely until it wears off, so no one can vote more than once. And as people left, picking up on the *fiesta política,* they waved a purple thumbs-up sign as a badge of civic honor. It is a wonderful custom, yet Costa Ricans are so scrupulous about these things that in recent years the Supreme Tribunal for Elections has been considering whether to change the process, because the obvious purple stain could be construed as an invasion of privacy.

Arias attended mass the morning of election day, breakfasted with the press, lunched with his parents at their home in San Joaquin, and, of course, voted. The early indications were blowing in the wind, as the green and white flags of Liberación seemed to outnumber the red and blue of the opposition. But that was by no means conclusive; there was still much uncertainty when the polls closed at 6 PM.

As the returns began to trickle in, it soon became clear that Calderón was in trouble. Arias's strategy had worked convincingly. The old Liberación strongholds in the countryside had been augmented by new strength in the cities built on Arias's appeal to the urban middle class. Arias dominated San José, Alajuela, Heredia, and Cartago, the "big four" of the Central Plateau. Calderón won by small margins in Limón and Puntarenas, economically depressed port towns of the Atlantic and Pacific where the status quo had not served well. And Arias held onto a slim lead in Guanacaste Province to the northwest. In round numbers, Arias would win 620,000 votes to Calderón's 542,000, 52 percent to 46 percent, with lesser parties (mainly Communist) accounting for 2 percent.

It was a tight race, one of the closest in twenty years. The turnout had been a record high both in terms of raw numbers and as a percentage of the population. The general impression was that Arias had won going away, that his strength had been building through the campaign, that the race had been masterfully, strategically run. And, best of all, Costa Rica's strong democratic tradition had been reaffirmed. There had been no violence, no polling disruptions, and not even the faintest whiff of tampering.

Election night found Oscar Arias, president-elect of Costa Rica, both jubilant and somber, as suited his style. He chose to quote Robert Frost, the quintessential New Englander, as he pondered the campaign as a beginning, not an end; "But I have promises to keep, and miles to go before I sleep, and miles to go before I sleep."

187

CHAPTER EIGHT

The Making of a Peace Plan

"I have always said that the worst enemy of democracy is cynicism and hypocrisy," Arias was saying, eight months into his term, sitting in the inner presidential office, explaining why he felt his campaign promises had to be taken with total seriousness. "I made a lot of pledges and commitments to Costa Rica, and in order to fulfill those commitments, we must maintain our *peace*."

"Everything rests upon it," he continued. "We cannot increase investments in Costa Rica, both from Costa Ricans and foreigners, if there is a war in Nicaragua." The stream of refugees strains the very fabric of the society. Entrepreneurs are not willing to take risks, to work with government to create the jobs and housing Arias promised. The incredible burden of the international debt cannot be renegotiated. "So the consequences of the civil war in Nicaragua for my country are awful, very damaging."

All of this demands that Costa Rica stay out of the wars of the region and do everything it can to bring about a peaceful resolution. This is usually referred to as "neutrality," but, as Arias said, "perhaps that's not the most appropriate word. We want to be neutral in the military conflicts of the region, but not neutral ideologically. That's not so. We totally identify with Western values, democracy, and what the United States represents. I have said that there will be no perpetual peace, long-term, in Central America, unless there are democratic governments. It is a prerequisite. And this view may not be shared by everybody. They may say, 'Why not peace without democracy?' I say that won't last. It must be peace *with* democracy."

The rhetoric is most interesting because it makes a hardheaded case for the idealistic values most people would like to apply. But it has been the action in support of the rhetoric that has elevated Arias. The first signs that he was a different brand of politician were not very long in coming.

Arias first began to assert his vision in February 1986— the same month as the election and more than two months before his inauguration. The occasion was an interview on national public television in the United States. The subject was the $100 million that the Reagan administration had convinced Congress to approve to support the contras in Nicaragua. And Arias's perspective was simple and clear: $100 million would do many more people much more good if it were spread around Central America as economic aid rather than put in the hands of the contras.

To be so blunt and direct with criticism is not a Costa Rican trait to begin with—although people would soon learn that Oscar Arias is atypical in his willingness to confront issues head-on. But to level such a clear castigation of United States foreign policy seemed almost heretical. People were shocked. The lame duck Costa Rican President Monge would soon express concern that Arias's outspokenness might jeopardize U.S. economic aid— Monge's main reason for being a virtual yes-man to an increasing military presence in the country over the previous four years.

It was not an idle concern. Costa Rica's foreign debt in 1983 was $3.5 billion; by 1985, it was $4.6 billion. In 1986, U.S. foreign aid to Costa Rica reached $325 million, half of it from the Agency for International Development (AID). Yet the money was not pulling Costa Rica out of the quicksand: In 1986, the foreign debt had reached the level of 90 percent of the gross domestic product. This figure does not compare with the debt of countries like Brazil and Mexico, but per capita it is the largest of the region, more than two thousand dollars for every Costa Rican. The interest payments alone are enough to hamstring an economy.

All of this implies that the prosperity and security of Costa Rica are something of a mirage. What seems to be a successful Third World free-enterprise culture is actually a society living far beyond its means. Cuba and Nicaragua may need Soviet aid to exist, but they presumably don't give advice to the Soviets about how to spend their money and conduct foreign policy. The United States itself has a serious balance of payments problem, but when your country is receiving the equivalent of a million dollars a day in U.S. aid, you might want to be circumspect about how hard you slap the hand that feeds. As if to underscore the precariousness of the situation, soon after Arias's comments, $25 million in AID money from the United States was suddenly delayed. It was hard to believe that this was sheer coincidence.

One heartening sign was that both Venezuela and Colombia jumped to support Arias. But Elliott Abrams, the undersecretary of state who would become known as the point man for much of the Reagan administration's policy in Central America, announced, "I simply believe Arias is mistaken." By April, Abrams was hotly denying reports that economic pressure was being exerted on Arias to fall in line with contra support. As it turned out, Abrams would lie to Congress about this subject in the months ahead.

But the effect of all this was to keep expectations about the Arias presidency very modest. On inauguration day, May 8, as he became the forty-eighth president of Costa Rica, Arias chose to speak mainly about peace and foreign affairs. He promised to keep Costa Rica out of the wars that plague Central America. He promised to use all diplomatic and political means to prevent "Central American brothers" from killing each other. He warned that "it is foolish to confuse dialogue with weakness." He surveyed history and announced that dictatorships were forms of the past, that democracy represented the present and future. He quoted Costa Rican poet Jorge Debravo, saying, "Brick by brick, man by man, we will create the world all over again."

No doubt it was purely unintentional, but the quote harkened back to the words John Kennedy spoke in San

José twenty-three years earlier. "We will build a wall around Cuba," Kennedy had proclaimed, "a wall of dedicated men . . ." Arias's sense of dedication and anti-Communism was more humanistic and positive, less fearful. "It is more important to build bridges that unite," Arias had said after winning the election, "than walls that divide."

Arias's thinking about domestic politics clearly reflected the idea of consensus-building. He bypassed the old system of making political appointments strictly from within the party hierarchy, reaching out for bipartisan support. The government that took shape was extremely young: Arias himself was only forty-five; the minister of agriculture was in his twenties; and the oldest vice-minister was less than fifty. It was a personal government: When Arias wanted to make sure that the police force was under control, he brought in his younger brother Rodrigo to be minister of security. He rewarded allies and sought out competence at the same time. Guido Fernandez, who crossed party lines to join Arias after the primary, soon became ambassador to the United States, while Otton Solis, only thirty-two years old, wooed back from England, became minister of planning. Arias drew on intellectuals and educators more than party hacks, and so, once more, a Kennedy style was emulated—this time in the form of a new generation of university people arriving at the house of government.

There were other examples that Arias was not about to follow. Within days of his inauguration, he made it quite clear that Ferdinand Marcos, fleeing from revolution in the Philippines, would find no home in Costa Rica. Figueres could welcome Vesco, but Arias was not going to welcome a dictator, no matter how much the United States might have liked to see Marcos settled.

Yet neither would Arias turn his back on Figueres and the Figueres legacy. There was pressure on the new president to dissociate himself from Figueres, who some felt had become a liability and an embarrassment—not to mention that Don Pepe had opposed Don Oscar in the primary. Arias thought it over for some time, swallowed whatever animosity he may have felt, and accorded Figueres more public respect than virtually anyone on the political scene. He emphasized Don Pepe's greatness as opposed to his petty corruption, he set about creating a national holiday of the day of the army's abolition, and when the Nobel Prize was announced, Don Pepe would be one of the people invited by Arias to accompany him to Oslo for the ceremony.

But the measure of the new president's mettle would really be tested when he received threats from the basement of the White House in Washington, D.C. And the crux of it would be whether a secret airstrip carved out of the Costa Rican jungle to service contra supply planes flying in and out of Nicaragua would be allowed to operate.

The strip, over a mile of nothing but flat dirt and grassland, had been hacked into existence beginning in 1985. It was located near the old hacienda and national park at Santa Rosa, the historic battleground of Costa Rican independence in Guanacaste Province. Even more ironic, before the fall of Nicaraguan dictator Anastasio Somoza, his family had owned much of the land in that remote northwestern corner of Costa Rica. According to a Costa Rican government report released years later, fifty civil guardsmen, headed by the local regional commander, had provided the manpower, on instructions from the CIA. And according to the official U.S. Tower Commission report, "contragate" characters Richard Secord and Albert Hakim supposedly provided $5 million to get the strip built—although there is no conceivable way that $5 million worth of work was done on that project. (This is a place where people work for a few dollars a day, and the biggest local payoff anyone heard about was a $15,000 car for the regional commander in charge. If $5 million were involved, the money went elsewhere.)

At any event, it turns out that Arias's predecessor, Luis Alberto Monge, would admit in coming months that he knew about, and approved of, the airstrip's construction. Monge told *The Tico Times* that U.S. officials had claimed they needed the runway to bolster Costa Rica's defense in the event Nicaragua invaded, which was in their opinion a possibility. Monge agreed in that context, he said, although the implication of economic blackmail hung heavy in the air during the entire Monge term. Every time Monge agreed to allow U.S. military personnel and advanced weaponry into northern Costa Rica, it seemed that more U.S. aid of all kinds came forward. And Monge's credibility about his motives was not helped by an indictment against him, charging the former president with siphoning public funds into a private account for his personal use.

Into this Pandora's box stepped Arias, and if ever there were a direct challenge to his campaign promise to strive for peace through democracy, this was it. "When I was elected," Arias remembers, "I was told there was this airstrip in the north, and that with the complacency of our government officials, the United States was offering logistic support to the contras. I told Mr. Lewis Tambs [then

U.S. ambassador to Costa Rica] that from now on, that would be changed. I would never accept that. I asked him to close the airstrip and stop all logistic support to the contras."

Forceful language, yet apparently Arias did not produce immediate results. Although Arias claims to have known about the airstrip shortly after his election, in February 1986, by September 1986, Oliver North was still stressing the importance of the Santa Elena "Point West" operation to John Poindexter. In a memo, North called the airfield "a vital element in supporting the resistance." He explained that the landing area had been used for "direct resupply efforts" to the contras from July 1985 through February 1986. Since then, it had become "the primary abort base for aircraft damaged by Sandinista anti-aircraft fire."[23] It seemed as though Arias's original protests may have changed the function of the landing field, but not closed it down.

By September 1986, however, Arias clearly had had enough. According to documents released in the Tower Commission report, the Costa Rican government had concluded that a public press conference should be held to reveal the existence of Santa Elena (perhaps with the motive to stop its operation once and for all). It was show-down time for Arias: Costa Rica would not allow itself to be drawn into the conflicts of the region, he had promised, and now Costa Rican soil was being used to open a southern front against the Sandinistas. This could not go on without the president losing all credibility.

On September 9, the strong-arm tactics from Washington became intense. According to memos released by the Tower Commission, Oliver North, Lewis Tambs, and Elliott Abrams all placed calls to Arias in a carefully orchestrated campaign, beginning with North. North's point was simple: If you hold that press conference and reveal the existence of the airstrip, $80 million of United States aid to Costa Rica will be cut off, and your invitation to come to Washington to meet President Reagan will be withdrawn. The message was supported in succeeding telephone conversations with Tambs and Abrams.

It was out-and-out blackmail, and North knew it. At the end of September he wrote to his superior, John Poindexter, as follows: "I recognize that I was well beyond my charter in dealing with a head of state this way and in making threats/offers that may be impossible to deliver but under the circumstances—and with Elliott's concurrence—it seemed like the only thing we could do."[24]

Poindexter's response: "You did the right thing, but let's try to keep it quiet."[25]

Whether Arias did the right thing, at least in the short run, is less clear. The press conference was canceled. He backed off public exposure. It seemed as though he had knuckled under. Yet consider this: By late September 1986, the airstrip had been discovered by both the Costa Rican and the United States press. There had been no press conference, yet somehow the word had gotten out. There was even some foolish talk by a Costa Rican official that the strip had been built to help promote "tourism"— simple geography made the idea patently absurd. Meanwhile, the strip had definitely, finally, stopped functioning: Logs and stumps were strewn along the way, and a contingent of guardsmen made sure they were not removed. There were international reports that children from San José had gone to the airstrip and planted trees there in symbolic protest. (The reports were not true.)

It looked like Arias had been able to have his cake and

eat it too. United States aid had not been disrupted and Arias still had his White House invitation, yet the airstrip had been closed and Costa Rica's neutrality had been asserted. His combination of pragmatism and vision, stubbornness and idealism, had managed to find a way.

And when the president showed up in Guanacaste Province the next July 25, 1987, to celebrate the anniversary of the area's annexation to Costa Rica, he was able to spread a little icing on top of his cake: The protected boundaries of the national park headquartered at Santa Rosa were about to be expanded by a good fifty square miles to help revive the region's tropical dry forest. Maybe it was coincidence that within those fifty square miles were the remains of the secret airstrip. Maybe it was coincidence that much of this area, now ceded to the Costa Rican people, had once been owned by Somoza. Maybe the annexation was strictly for conservation and environmental protection. Then again, maybe the art of Costa Rican symbolism was not mastered only by Don Pepe Figueres. Whatever way you look at it, the moment certainly provided a poignant postscript to "Point West."

Lewis Tambs turned out to be a casualty of the Point West confrontation. Tambs had arrived as ambassador to Costa Rica from Colombia, where conventional wisdom said that he had played a key role in busting up some major cocaine distribution schemes. It was said that the drug lords had put a price on his head, and so the transfer to Costa Rica was as much for his safety as anything. If that was the motivation, the choice of location seemed odd, since Costa Rica had become an important middle point in the cocaine trade.

At any event, by his own admission Tambs had been deeply involved in the "southern front" that the secret airstrip represented. And by December 1986, Tambs had resigned as ambassador, returning to university teaching in Arizona. As reported by NBC Nightly News on December 8, Tambs apparently delivered an ultimatum to the Arias government: Either supply better assistance to the contras, or I quit. Clearly Tambs had not made a good study of Arias. As Tom Brokaw said simply, "Costa Rica's government refused."

By June 1987, Arias would have his White House meeting with President Reagan. The Costa Rican president's independence had become a matter of some concern in Washington. Most galling to Reagan's people was Arias's consistent refusal to include the contras among the players in the diplomatic board game he was trying to fashion in Central America. This was still two months before the peace plan would emerge that would bear Arias's name, but already the direction of Costa Rica's foreign policy was unmistakable. Arias's close friend and adviser John Biehl accompanied the president to the White House and later told American journalists that it was "very scary stuff." *People Magazine* quoted Biehl as saying, "The Oval Office was filled with all the big boys, and Oscar appeared like Spartacus going before the Roman generals."[26]

Yet by all accounts Arias, his stubborn streak intact, would not budge. He told Reagan face to face what he had been saying for months: The contras are a part of the problem, not the solution. When Reagan obviously remained unconvinced, Arias was undaunted, adding only that he hoped to have another opportunity to be more eloquent with his argument. One unconfirmed, perhaps apocryphal, story circulating in Costa Rica was that as soon as Arias left the Oval Office, President Reagan was heard to explode, "Who let that midget in here?"

On the streets of San José, a more relaxed sense of the man has emerged. His low-key, accessible style suits the country and makes him among the least paranoid chief executives in the world. His home, a modest suburban house located a few blocks from La Sabana Park on a main residential street, did not even have a gate in front of the door for months after he was elected. His book-strewn study, where he likes to spend evenings reading and ruminating, has a big window that looks out on the street. It is not unusual to see the president driving through San José at the wheel of his jeep, or at lunch at a downtown restaurant, talking politics, his back to the plate glass window. The Ariases often show up at the theater or at concerts. Many people have stories about bumping into Arias at unexpected moments, like the young Costa Rican student flying to McGill University in Canada to resume his studies who suddenly realized that the president of his country was the only other person sitting in that section of the plane. "I'm buying my friend a beer," said Arias, and the two of them talked through the flight. Arias bridles at suggestions to be more security-conscious, more remote, more a prisoner of his office. And yet, as one Costa Rican official confirmed, the president receives his share of anonymous, threatening phone calls.

Avoiding pretense and maintaining a sense of perspective are Costa Rican national traits people appreciate in a president. Yet in other ways Don Oscar has not been typically Costa Rican. For example, it is in the nature of Costa Rica to avoid direct confrontation, verbal or physical. And Costa Ricans have become accustomed to their leaders adopting a similar posture. The president before Arias, Monge, was a master, as one official put it, "of a no-policy policy. He turned it into an art." In Germany, they call this the *"ja-nein"* idea of politics, meaning *ja* and *nein,* yes and no, all at once. In Costa Rica they say *"más o menos,"* more or less, or even *"sí pero no,"* the yes-but-no school of diplomacy. Yet Arias prides himself on being very forthright, on saying yes and meaning yes, on saying no and meaning no. In a democracy like Costa Rica's, where institutional checks and balances are so strong that paralysis can set in, an executive willing to stick his neck out can be a very positive force.

Arias has also developed an image of intellectual spontaneity. Whether it was carefully designed or the simple truth is tough to tell, but it seems to work to his advantage. A *New York Times* correspondent recalled to a colleague his amazement when Oscar Arias phoned out of the blue mainly to shoot the breeze and talk about his thoughts on rereading *The Ballad of Reading Gaol* by Oscar Wilde. Calls like that tend to bear the fruit of sympathetic coverage.

Yet ulterior motives do not seem to be necessary for his philosophizing. Even in the midst of intense negotiations about the peace process, Arias would take time out to muse with me about the roots of Costa Rican democracy, to deliver a professorial lecture on the evolution of Costa Rican land use, and then to dismiss the common analogy that Costa Rica is the Switzerland of Central America. "We want to be the Denmark of Central America, not Switzerland," he said with all earnestness. "My paradigm would be Denmark, because it is both politically democratic and economically democratic, with small property owners, well-distributed small industries, and lots of cooperatives." Did you know, he pushed on, that Costa Rica has the largest cooperative movement in Latin America? "Eleven percent of the GNP."

This emphasis on cooperatives would become a cornerstone of the government's domestic policy. By early 1988, according to Minister of Planning and Economic Policy Otton Solis, 550 Costa Rican cooperatives were employing 260,000 members out of a 900,000-person labor force. Forty-five percent of the national exports emerged from cooperatives, with the best successes in coffee, sugar, beef, and milk processing.

Solis waxes eloquent about why Arias places so much importance on cooperatives, which can best be described as worker-owned businesses in which profit, far from being a dirty word, is as welcome as in any capitalist sweatshop. "The important thing," says Solis, "is that cooperatives represent the best solution between the dilemma of efficiency versus justice. It's the root of the most important ideological debate in the world. Unadulterated capitalists talk about efficiency and production as opposed to social justice, but the cooperative philosophy works in Costa Rica because it melts away that distinction. It uses private incentives, yet avoids inequality."

At the heart of Costa Rica's envious position in Central America, Solis argues, "has been a capacity to keep an eye on justice without forgetting efficiency. If you only care about justice, you don't wind up with justice. Look at Nicaragua. But if you look only at efficiency, you get into the destructive schemes of El Salvador, Iran, you name it."

Meanwhile, the twin pillars of promise in Arias's campaign, jobs and housing, were being addressed in ways that seemed to fuse the two. For starters, the government used a bit of fancy semantics to help reach the campaign goal of twenty thousand new homes a year. The phrase *housing solutions* was substituted for *new homes,* which meant that renovations, remodeling, and all kinds of improvements could substitute for brand-new buildings. Critics charge that this is tampering with truth, and their criticism rings true. But even so, according to Solis, over 80 percent of the 21,700 new houses accounted for during the first year of the Arias administration were constructions, not "solutions." Throughout San José in particular, bulldozers seem to be churning foundation holes in every other vacant lot, and many a squatter's shack has been knocked down, the slums transformed into single-family homes.

"Housing has become a crusade, a fashion," says Solis, and he has a point. "When a country is able to make the fashion of the time something constructive like housing, something positive rather than nationalistic hatred, or antagonism, that's the most powerful thing."

The government has been implementing the "fashion" with a carrot-and-stick approach, making it clear that applications for business loans or other capital projects would certainly be helped along if new housing is built into the package. Higher taxes, which Arias has pushed through the Costa Rican Congress, have seemed palatable in large part because support for public housing projects is so strong. "Now it is not impossible," says Arias, "to dream of Costa Rica as the first slum-free Central American nation before the year 2000." Make that the first slum-free nation in the world. And make the dream, while closer to reality than anywhere else in Central America, still remote.

The double benefit of a housing crusade is that the building trade is so labor-intensive that it creates many new jobs. One policy, two objectives. Costa Rica has never been known to have what economists refer to as "good productivity ratios," meaning that the number of people employed seems high for the amount of work they do. But in developing countries, people worry foremost about whether there are jobs at all, and the combination of domestic construction with higher coffee quotas, such new agricultural products as macadamia nuts, flowers, and strawberries, plus ever more favorable conditions for foreign investors has convinced most everyone that the new jobs Arias promised are actually out there.

Solis does admit to "distorted elements" of the economy, particularly regarding the lack of satisfying work for well-trained professionals, and the constraints on upward mobility for women. The government now has a guaranteed loan program for women-run business, but the national goals in this regard are very modest. "We want ten projects created with women in rural areas of Costa Rica," says Solis. The projects he has in mind are processing jams and packing eggs or flowers.

Working with these nuts and bolts of domestic economics is not the glamor side of government, not the work that galvanizes foreign correspondents or puts a president in line for the Nobel Peace Prize. Of course it is crucial stuff, and Arias understands this well: If there is one thing Costa Ricans cling to more than anything else, it is expectations for yet more and yet better. Governments that do not offer that hope are governments that fail, and failing governments cannot spend their time fashioning creative international diplomacy.

Yet Arias clearly is drawn to the world theater, and his presidency reflects that bias. He argues that peace is the crucial prerequisite for economic growth, which is true, but the argument also justifies the preoccupation he would incline toward anyway.

One interesting insider in the Arias government who

has moved foreign policy forward, a *carpintero,* to use the tico term, is Luis Guillermo Solis, chief of staff of the ministry of foreign affairs. Luis Guillermo is no relation to Otton Solis ("He's one of the rich Solises," laughs Luis Guillermo), but they are similar in some ways: Young, intellectual, also pulled out of academia into the public sector, this Solis was schooled partly in the United States and has a picture of Abraham Lincoln hanging over his desk. He has written a book called *Subjects or Allies? U.S. Foreign Policy and Central America,* a political history that touches that most tender nerve—the ambivalence Latins feel toward the United States. Since he arrived in the Arias government, he has focused on drawing Europeans into Central American diplomacy, a tactic designed to counterbalance the force of United States economic and geographic dominance.

The Arias government hit the ground running with its foreign policy. In May 1986, as heads of state were arriving for Arias's inauguration, several key pieces of what would become known as the Arias Peace Plan were already being assembled. Luis Guillermo remembers that a timetable for reforms was on the table, and Arias's people were so sure of what they were doing that they seriously considered using the inauguration as an excuse to hold a summit right then and there, while the various bigshots were in San José. "The idea was rejected," Solis recalls, "only because it was not the appropriate moment or setting."

After only a few months on the job, Solis accompanied his immediate superior, Foreign Minister Rodrigo Madrigal, on a crucial trip to Europe. They took with them a handful of ideas, some old and some new, which formed the basis of the Arias idea of diplomacy. "We were requesting a suspension of aid [to the contras]," remembers Solis. "That was old. But simultaneity was a new thing, the simultaneous application of all parts of the agreement we could fashion. Of course a timetable was important. And, foremost really, democratization."

Buzzwords like *democratization* had been bandied about Central America for so long, without a great deal of good faith, that Europeans were fundamentally suspicious. When the press reported on what was supposed to be a confidential meeting with United States officials in Miami before the European trip, it made the Costa Ricans look, in Solis's words, "like we were getting our orders, not giving our ideas. We feel it was leaked by someone in the State Department, in [Elliott] Abrams's office."

Despite a rough start, Solis and Madrigal spent three weeks barnstorming Europe, moving from Spain to Great Britain, Germany, France, Austria, and Belgium. They met the Pope in Rome. They talked to the radical Greens in Germany and Waldheim in Vienna, to businessmen, journalists, and parliaments. The overriding idea was to develop credibility for Costa Rica and support for democracy in Central America.

"Several conclusions emerged from that trip," Solis remembers. "First, the contras were receiving *no* public or private support. It was totally untrue what the United States government was saying, that Europeans were saying one thing in public, and another in private. There was simply no support for them.

"Second, there was great disenchantment with the Sandinistas in most countries and political groups, except in the groups of left-wing socialists in Germany or Spain. The situation had totally changed since the previous June. . . . Enacting and then suspending the Constitution had hurt them tremendously. All their public relations had turned against them. Expectations had been so high that disappointment was great." Yet neither did the Contadora group, composed of pro-U.S. governments in Latin America, have much credibility in Europe.

So the European stage was set for exactly the kind of character Arias could play: A leading man with integrity and independence, schooled in the western values of democracy and free enterprise, without national scandal and corruption turning his words into empty platitudes. And while United States thinkers tend to discount what people in Brussels, Spain, or Austria might think, the Europeans' impressions gave the Arias foreign policy a community of support, a moral legitimacy that needed to be affirmed.

But the drama could unfold only in Central America. By February 1987, a year after his election, Arias was circulating the outline of his peace plan for the region. Its crucial point, from the very beginning, was that every Central American nation must restore full democracy and freedom of the press. In return, all outside aid to rebels in the region would cease and governments would be obliged to negotiate only with unarmed groups within their borders.

Cynics said that the plan was typical of Costa Rica's national mentality: When in doubt, try to make everybody else look and act as much like Costa Rica as possible. And skeptics had no optimism that an Arias plan, soon to be denounced by the Reagan administration as "fatally flawed" because it accepted the existence of the Sandinista government, would have any more success than the Contadora group's futile efforts over the previous three years.

But the strange thing about the Arias Peace Plan is that

it took on many of the characteristics of the man whose name it bore. Dogged, stubborn, underestimated yet tougher than anyone thought, the plan withstood months of bricks and barbs. Its fundamental trade-off—real democracy for nonintervention—was a policy neither the United States nor the Sandinistas could dismiss, because to have dismissed it would have turned either of them into hypocrites. All along, the United States had been saying (publicly at least) that what it wanted in Nicaragua was not a puppet but a democracy. And all along, the Sandinistas had been saying (publicly at least) that the only thing that was stopping them from being a real democracy was a state of war created by United States interference. So Arias said, stop the aid, hold real elections, and let the chips fall where they may.

By the time the five Central American presidents gathered at the Camino Real Hotel in Guatemala City on August 6 and 7, 1987, it is fair to say that there were no great expectations. Meetings had been held before, pacts had been discussed and even signed before, and nothing seemed to have changed. The press was predicting little. Arias, serious and almost pessimistic, arrived in Guatemala repeating words he had been saying over the previous few months, aimed mainly at Nicaragua's President Daniel Ortega: "In democratic systems, everything that is not prohibited is permitted, while in totalitarian systems, everything that is not permitted is prohibited. These two visions of the world do not easily coexist."

Indeed, in some ways the meeting would hinge on how Arias and Ortega would confront each other. Arias had some credibility in Nicaragua; after all, not only had he closed the contra airstrip, but the founder of his political party, José Figueres, had been an ardent supporter of the revolution. And it was crucial that Arias maintain his growing credibility in the United States and Europe, which was built on his unswerving belief in democracy. So, as reliable accounts have it, almost as soon as the five presidents convened in their hotel suite, José Napoleon Duarte from El Salvador, José Azcona from Honduras, Vinicio Cerezo from Guatemala, Arias, and Ortega, a little confrontation occurred. Arias singled out Ortega and asked him in front of the rest whether he was *really* ready to sit down and negotiate some hard issues. If not, Arias reportedly told him, let's not waste a lot of time and energy, let's shoot the breeze for a while, go out for the cameras, smile and wave, and go home. But if so, then let's get down to business.

It established a tone, it put Ortega on the spot, and it made Arias appear hardheaded, willing to give and take, and looking for real results. As the meeting carried on through the day of August 6, Arias began to feel that they were close to something momentous. The dinner hour approached and momentum continued, but people were hungry and wanted to break for some food. Arias is fond of recalling that a passage from a biography of Franklin Roosevelt came to mind, describing a tactic Roosevelt employed to get his advisers to reach a consensus on a difficult question: He'd lock them in the room until they had come to terms with each other. Arias suggested room service to keep them all at the table, and the meeting continued.

It wasn't until 4 AM the next day, Friday, August 7, that Arias walked out of that hotel suite. He had what he had been searching for across more than one continent, what he had promised Costa Rican voters he would try to find: a peace plan for Central America.

The ideas that made their way into the Guatemala accords included some things borrowed, some things old, and some things new:

- Amnesty would safeguard life and freedom in all five countries, and irregular armies would simultaneously free all people in their custody.

- A dialogue with any group that accepts the amnesty provision would be set up by the government in question.

- A ceasefire "within the constitutional framework" would be accomplished by "all necessary action."

- Every government would agree to "promote an authentic, pluralist and democratic process of participation," which would include "complete freedom for television, radio, and the press . . . full political party pluralism," and the end of any emergency decrees or martial law.

- As soon as this is done, "free, pluralist, and honest elections shall have to be held for representatives of a Central American Parliament" in every country. Outside observers would be allowed to see that the elections were in every way open.

- At the same time, the five governments would do everything in their power to stop anyone from "openly or secretly provid[ing] military, logistic, financial, promotional, human resources, armaments, ammunitions, and equipment aid to the irregular forces or to the rebels."

- None of the countries would allow their territory to be used to help destabilize other governments.

- An international committee of verification would follow the progress of the accord, which would have a series of deadlines that must be met to keep all the countries in compliance.

It wasn't everything, but it surely was something. In some ways it was very legalistic and detailed, but in other ways it was very vague and toothless—for instance, no sanctions were spelled out for countries that did not comply with the terms. Arias, clearly elated and exhausted, saw the document both as the culmination of months of effort—and as a beginning.

The people of Costa Rica saw the signing as a triumph. Church bells rang through the country on August 7, cars honked their horns. "They signed!" people yelled out of car windows. When Arias returned over the weekend, crowds met and mobbed him. Let people mutter about Neville Chamberlain and appeasement. Let Ronald Reagan talk about a "fatal flaw." And let worries about compliance wait for the months ahead. For a nation increasingly nervous about war spilling over its border, for people who had been feeling more and more isolated and threatened, who felt their freedom and security in jeopardy, the peace plan was a wonderful victory both of diplomacy and spirit. Their president had allowed Costa Ricans to breathe a deep, collective sigh of relief.

CHAPTER NINE

The Meaning of the Nobel

To be nominated for the Nobel Peace Prize was certainly an honor for Oscar Arias, but it was nothing new for Costa Rica. In the past decade the nation has been nominated a handful of times, mainly in recognition of the abolition of the army. That it had never won was no reflection on the country, but more an indication that the Nobel committees seem to use the prize to honor individuals and institutions, not cultures, and to try to invest efforts to untie Gordian knots of violence in the world with esteem and credibility. Desmond Tutu in South Africa in 1984, Lech Walesa in Poland in 1983, and Anwar Sadat and Menachem Begin in the Middle East in 1978 are all such recipients of the prize. Because Elie Wiesel, an author and scholar, had won the prize in 1986 for his writings on the Holocaust, preceded by the Physicians for the Prevention of Nuclear War in 1985, it seemed a political figure was due for recognition.

There were ninety-three candidates before the committee in 1987, and Oscar Arias was not generally considered to be a front-runner. Most pundits predicted that Corazon Aquino, whose relatively peaceful revolution had led the Philippines past Marcos, would take the prize. Terry Waite, the courageous minister and negotiator who had vanished in Lebanon while trying to get hostages freed, was another leading candidate. Even the Dalai Lama, clinging to his religious vision of a Tibet free from Chinese control, seemed a more likely choice.

But on October 13, 1987, two months after the peace agreement was signed, a month before the first of the deadlines for progress spelled out by the accord, the world learned that the winner was Oscar Arias Sánchez, President of Costa Rica.

In retrospect, it was a brilliant choice. Aquino's position had become less clear, less obviously principled, in the months since she assumed office. And if leverage for peace was what the Nobel committee wanted to exert, anointing Arias while the peace plan was still birthing was good strategy. Almost immediately, two things happened: First, Arias was suddenly endowed with a status described by some as "papal," his name now invoked with righteous fervor. "Prior to the Arias Nobel Peace Prize, it was a question of whether Ortega screwed up," U.S. House Democratic Whip Tony Coehlo told *Newsweek*. "Today it's a question of what Arias thinks."[27] And second, the Reagan administration, so busy wiping egg off its face about the Iran-contra connection, had to stop sniping at the man and the plan.

Back in San José, even longtime friends and supporters couldn't believe the turn of events. Months earlier they had joked about Arias's vaulting ambition, how he acted as if he had been born to be president, how he had been rumored to say that he wanted to win the Nobel Peace Prize and then become secretary general of the United Nations. Now it was two out of three, before the age of fifty. People credited him with determination, vision, and something else as well. "You can consider Oscar as a classic case of a man with great good luck," said Carmen Naranjo, former minister of culture, one of Costa Rica's most insightful observers. Yet again a cultural trait, this time that elusive luck that seems to hover over Costa Rica, had transmigrated into the president.

Arias and his family reportedly were relaxing on the Pacific coast when the prize was announced. As the tempo of his life was about to double, this was probably fortunate. He raced back to the capital, greeted with nearly universal hosannas, his name chanted from the seats of the National Theater and the sidewalks of Avenida Central. "This is one of the happiest days of my life," he said. "The jury recognized what we Costa Ricans have been doing for many years: trying to bring peace to the region." He tried to direct the award toward the other presidents who signed the accord, to say it was "a response to their rationality." He insisted that it was an award for all of Costa Rica. Actually, in fact as well as emotion, it was Oscar Arias's prize.

Yet as is so often the case with Central American events, the Arias Nobel Peace Prize also revealed much

about the United States, the way light from an unexpected angle reveals much about an object. More than
anything, it served to expose what United States allies like
Costa Rica have long seen as a U.S. schizophrenia: a
handsome, craggy profile of domestic intentions that, in
Jekyll and Hyde fashion, often turns into a grotesque, distorted mask of foreign policy.

In domestic affairs, the United States is the envy and
inspiration of much of the world for its democracy and its
access. Even amid all our inequalities and failures there is
a sense that our sluggish government does bend to the
will of the people, does respond to political pressure of
the left and right, does recognize principles of fairness and
the people's legitimate needs. All of this is most imperfect
in its unfolding; still, it is probably closer to perfect than
anywhere else in the world.

Yet our foreign policy often distorts these values. The
litany of our allies since World War Two includes some
appalling characters: Batista, Trujillo, Somoza, Duvalier,
Noriega, Pinochet—and that is only a sampling of one
hemisphere, one generation. These dictators have scorned
democracy and due process, the cornerstones of the
United States domestic policy, yet we support them. And
so the United States has come to represent both the greatest promise and worst evil, the standard of freedom and
the buttress of brutality.

Why is it that the ideals we cherish at home are the
very ideals our Third World allies repress? Are we so gul-
lible that a dictator can simply pronounce the words
"Communist subversives" and we immediately send him
all the weapons he needs to crush his country and enrich
his family?

The best way to understand the apparent schizophrenia

is to appreciate the underlying constant: The United States government responds to pressure. That is democracy's greatest strength. In the long run, people willing to organize, vote, lobby, and yell create the competing pressures that lead to compromise and decent public policy.

In domestic politics a lot of people yell about a lot of issues, from potholes in the street to racism on the job to favoritism in Congress. But in foreign policy there is no such immediacy. Until we get into a war, or a major public drama unfolds, the only people who care enough to create pressure to push government around are the people who stand to make or lose money from the resulting policy. By and large, that means multinational corporations. And when you appraise their motives coldly, what they care about is stability and an advantageous financial climate. Call it good capitalism or mean exploitation, but either way democracy and due process are not high on a checklist that emphasizes the bottom line. Democracy is uncertain. Human rights and free expression mean things like higher wages. The dictator may be cruel but he is a constant that can be understood; the price of corruption can be factored into the cost of doing business.

So the result is schizophrenic but the motive is always the same: Elected officials do what they feel they must to be re-elected. This is not necessarily cynical, this can mean good representation. At home, competing forces push for pluralism. But with Third World policy, where the constituency has historically been big business, the results don't always stand up to our social principles. As silly as it sounds, the fundamental truth is that Central Americans do not vote for United States politicians, which makes United States politicians less sensitive to their interests.

The awarding of the Nobel Peace Prize to Oscar Arias brought this into focus. The entire thrust of Arias's effort is based on the fundamental assumption that the United States ideal is alive in Latin America, that democracy and free expression are true goals and true cures, that cynicism and economic motivation are not the only calling cards of American diplomats. Clearly the Nobel Prize committee recognized this vision. They threw their support to Arias as if to say that, while President Reagan might choose to see the contras as "freedom fighters," the world at large sees efforts like Arias's as the kind of hand-to-hand combat that contributes to freedom and peace.

So, both Arias and Costa Rica were suddenly elevated and recognized. "When I used to talk about Costa Rica in England," remembers Otton Solis, "people would giggle. Who cared? Who cared if this little country doesn't have an army? But now, with the Nobel, people care."

Arias, ever the pragmatist, saw that the peace prize could do more than provide political support; it could be translated into money, too. His ministers began pushing harder for economic assistance, holding up the ideal of the society, arguing that aid for Costa Rica is aid for democracy, aid for the standard-bearer of Third World free enterprise with democracy. Within the Liberación Party, people were urging Arias, in the words of one party official, "to stop being the foreign minister, and get back to being the President." No, Arias argued in return, what you don't understand is that this Nobel Peace Prize is going to do more for our economy than anything else I could have accomplished. Party leaders left the meeting shaking their heads, thinking that Don Oscar had lost touch with reality.

Yet he was right again. For example, tourism in Costa

Rica, which had suffered severely because of the war in Nicaragua (down 16 percent in 1983, 7.7 percent in early 1984, and falling through 1985), suddenly picked up. Costa Rica is now a popular place to go; more travel articles have been written about its attractions in the past year than in the previous five. "Before the prize," remembers a tour guide who meets large cruise ships at the port of Limón and takes passengers on day trips around Costa Rica, "many of the people on the cruise didn't get off the boat. They were scared. They thought they might get shot. But now, everyone gets off, everyone wants to see peaceful Costa Rica. And everyone buys something." That attitude is multiplying and rippling through the economy. A young entrepreneur building a new country club near Quesada said, "The Nobel Prize was the greatest present ever given to the business community of Costa Rica," while even institutions like the World Bank seem inclined to give Costa Rica more favorable lending rates because the nation has become a symbol of how things ought to be done.

Meanwhile, the area where the prize has had the least influence, amazingly enough, has been in the local political arena. They say that prophets are never revered in their homelands; Arias's opinions seem to draw more unqualified support outside Costa Rica than inside the country or even in the Liberación Party. The general feeling, as one government official put it, is that "Oscar is going to have to get his hands dirty, he's going to have to get control of the party to accomplish what he wants at home. He's transcended; he's beyond good and evil. But the Nobel Peace Prize counts zip in domestic politics." And perhaps the best way to see this is to delve into the relationship between President Arias and *La Nación,* the leading daily newspaper of Costa Rica.

The first edition of *La Nación* rolled off the presses on October 12, 1946, two years before the Figueres revolution, funded mainly by wealthy Costa Ricans to be an opposition voice to the radical policies of Calderón and the Communists. When Figueres won and refused to lead Costa Rica back toward a conservative policy that favored the wealthier class, *La Nación's* editorial policy turned hard against him and Liberación. Throughout the years the hatred between Figueres and *La Nación* has been deep, far beyond politics. That opposition has extended to the party, which *La Nación* has invariably opposed, although the intensity of the clash is not always so bitterly personal.

Most people in Costa Rica see the press as very conservative and controlled by the rich. When a director of *La Nación* was confronted with his connections to a rightwing group that had paramilitary overtones called Costa Rica Libre, he told the interviewer, as recounted by one of his own reporters, "If we're the far right, then all of Costa Rica is far right."

Significant numbers of people in Costa Rica also see the press as manipulated by United States interests and manipulative of the public at large. Journalist Martha Honey argues that regular meetings between Costa Rican editors and United States Information Service personnel laid down the editorial line for the papers to follow. "There was a very concerted effort to use the press to turn Costa Rica against the Sandinistas," Honey believes. "And journalists were put on a payroll, either CIA or contra. The mission was to write pro-contra, anti-Nicaragua stuff."

Even respected liberal thinkers like Carmen Naranjo,

former minister of culture, agree. "If we speak sincerely, freedom of the press does not exist," she argues. "There are a series of means of communication with a monolithic position in which the U.S. government has great influence."

This is the sort of debate that might go on in the United States about the true meaning of "freedom of the press." In both countries, many people say that freedom of the press is guaranteed only to people who have enough money to own their own printing plant. The argument has some merit, but it is a far cry from government soldiers closing the office and seizing the publication. And there *is* diversity in Costa Rica: For example, the respected but small weekly, *The Tico Times*, written in English, is much more liberal than *La Nación*, and the former editor of *La Nación*, Guido Fernandez, has become Arias's ambassador to the United States. Another former reporter for the paper, Lidiette Brenes de Chapentier, is now head of Arias's press office. Foreign Minister Rodrigo Madrigal is a former director of *La Republica*, another daily. And Eduardo Ulibarri, present editor of *La Nación*, is generally described as extremely conservative but scholarly, reasoned in his position.

Yet there is little that could be described as scholarly in *La Nación*'s coverage of what must be seen as the most important symbolic achievement a Costa Rican president has accomplished in a generation. To be fair, Eduardo Ulibarri, the paper's editor, was in Cambridge, Massachusetts, at the time, on a leave of absence to pursue a Nieman fellowship. Moreover, Arias himself kicked things off on a negative note: Holding his last press conference before leaving to accept the Nobel Prize, speaking to reporters at Juan Santamaría airport on December 7, Arias blasted *La Nación* for what he called extreme right-wing attitudes and a misinterpretation of freedom of the press. Reading the paper, he said, "one would get the impression that in Costa Rica only bad things happen, because the good is ignored and not published."[28] It was a sour note on which to leave the country for such a prestigious ceremony, but it was indicative of how strained domestic politics had become.

Stopping in El Salvador, Guatemala, and New York for various discussions, Arias received the Nobel Prize in Norway on December 10. That day *La Nación* chose to publish two articles related to the prize (beyond a simple news announcement of the event). One, a full-page article on the front of an insert called "Viva," reminded Costa Ricans that in 1985 a Costa Rican doctor was among the Physicians to Prevent Nuclear War who received a peace prize. The clear implication of the article was: Remember that Arias isn't the first one to win a Nobel around here.[29]

The other article was the lead column on the editorial page, and it was titled *"Nuestros Dos Papás,"* Our Two Fathers.

"On Christmas Eve," it began, "Costa Ricans will have two fathers: Father Noël, and Father Nobel."

Father Noël will bring happiness with his gifts; Father Nobel will bring peace with taxes.

Father Noël will bring us gifts in a sack; Father Nobel will bring us a tax package.

Father Noël will barely squeeze through the door of customs; Father Nobel will stroll with room to spare through the diplomatic room.

The gifts of Father Noël come every year in a sleigh; the taxes of Father Nobel arrive each second by supersonic computer. . . .

Father Noël lives on a faraway star; Father Nobel
is now a star.

Father Noël isn't of this world; Father Nobel has
stopped being of this world. . . .

"Father Noël kisses many people; Many people
kiss Father Nobel."[30]

The writing was clever, particularly because people had
been referring to Arias as the "papa" of the peace plan,
meaning the maker as well as the father. But it was petty,
and it showed poor judgment. Even the following day,
December 11, when *La Nación* ran a big photo of Arias
accepting the peace prize, its front page also carried a
story about reactions to the United States–Russian arms
agreement as well as three headlines about problems and
investigations of domestic activity in Costa Rica. An inside
page was devoted to the awards, and Arias's speech was
reprinted (along with a cartoon that made him look both
apeish and foolish), but the editorial of the day was titled
"Rumbos paralelos," (Parallel paths). It concluded that the
very agreement Arias had helped fashion and that led to
the peace prize actually "has become a propaganda tool
for the left and a mask for the Sandinistas to show to the
world insincere gestures of peace."[31]

Once again, the journalistic judgment seemed horrendous. This was a time to drop partisan bickering and congratulate the president of the country. If that was too
bitter a pill to swallow, then perhaps Arias could have
been mildly praised for using the entire $340,000 of the
peace prize to establish a foundation to help poor people
in Costa Rica. If personal praise was out of the question,
perhaps some tribute could have been made to Costa Rica
during its shining moment in the international spotlight.

Using the occasion to blast the Arias peace plan as a left-wing dupe and deception was remarkably myopic and made Arias's airport tirade as he left to receive the prize more understandable.

This is the kind of nitty-gritty Arias has to deal with day in and day out, and which greeted him when he returned from Oslo. This is the kind of stuff he had to wade through to become president, and must wade through to continue to shape the course of his party, his government, and his country.

But the reason he was invited to Oslo had more to do with his vision than his stubbornness. As he accepted the Nobel Peace Prize on December 10, 1987, the day of his son's eighth birthday, Arias spoke only briefly, one of the shortest and least formal Nobel acceptance speeches in memory; it was less than eight hundred words. And he chose to speak in English, so he could be certain that the message he wanted to deliver would be understood by "them," by those countries in the East and the West that have become involved in Central America:

> I say to them, with the utmost urgency: Let Central Americans decide the future of Central America. Leave the interpretation and implementation of our peace plan to us. Support the efforts for peace instead of the forces of war in our region. Send our people ploughshares instead of swords, pruning hooks instead of spears. If they, for their own purposes, cannot refrain from amassing the weapons of war, then, in the name of God, at least they should leave us in peace.

The words were both appropriate and blunt, urging that the United States stop aid to the Nicaraguan rebels, and the Russians stop military aid to the Sandinistas. He meant to have political impact, and spoke in English so the speech could be broadcast on the evening news. The speech reflected Arias the pragmatist, making good use of a unique world podium to help move his diplomacy forward.

Yet at an evening dinner celebrating the awarding of the prize, Arias had an opportunity to speak poetically and at greater length of the vision that carried him to Norway. The speech he delivered was superb, Latin in its prose style, resonant in its choice of words. There is also a touch of formality, even stuffiness, about the tone, just as there can be about the man. But a passion reverberates through the language. Understanding something of Costa Rica, understanding something of the background and personality of Oscar Arias, makes the sentiments offered to the world that night that much more meaningful. Most important, it is the experience of the nation that makes the leader's words ring true and allows him the beauty and luxury of a moral platform from which to speak. A full translation by David Wood of the speech, as it appeared in *La Nación*, follows. There was at least one change in the delivery: José Figueres, though invited to attend the ceremonies, could not make the trip because of failing health. It must have saddened Figueres to miss this grand culmination of efforts that he in part encouraged, in part began.

"ONLY PEACE CAN WRITE A NEW HISTORY"

To Desire Peace

Peace consists, in large part, in desiring it with all one's soul. Those are the words of Erasmus which the people of my little Costa Rica live by. Mine is a country without arms, where our children have never seen a fighter plane, or a tank, or a warship. One of my invited guests to receive this prize, here with us, is José Figueres Ferrer, the visionary man who in 1948 abolished the army of my country and who showed, in so doing, a different direction for our history.

I Am a Latin American

I do not receive this prize as Oscar Arias. Nor do I receive it as the president of my country. I do not have the arrogance to pretend that I represent someone or something, but neither am I afraid of the humility that identifies me with all people, and with their grand causes.

I receive this prize as one of the 400 million Latin Americans who are looking to return to liberty, using the practice of democracy as the way to overcome so much misery and so much injustice. I am one of that Latin America whose face is marked with deep scars of pain, who remembers exile, torture, prison, and death of many of our men and women. I am of that Latin America whose geography still shows totalitarian regimes which shame all of humanity.

The Scars of America

The scars that mark America are deep. America is looking, in our years, to return to liberty, and when democracy shows itself, it sees first the horrible trail of torture, exile, and death which was left behind by the dictator. The problems which America must overcome are enormous. The inheritance of a past of injustices is aggravated by the nefarious action of a tyrant to produce external debt, social insensitivity, the destruction of the economy, corruption, and many other evils in our society. These ills can be seen, nakedly exposed, for anyone who wishes to look.

It is not strange that, before the magnitude of this challenge, many have given in to despair; that the prophets of the Apocalypse abound, those that announce the failures of the struggles against poverty, those who preach the incipient fall of democracies, those who predict the futility of the efforts for peace.

I do not share this defeatism. I am not able to accept that to be a realist means accepting misery, violence, and hatred. I do not believe that a man who is hungry, and expresses his pain, must be treated as a subversive. I will never be able to accept that the rule of law can be used to justify tragedy, to maintain the status quo, to stop thinking of a different world. The law is the way to liberty, and as such, is the opportunity for the development of all.

Liberty Makes Miracles

Liberty makes miracles. When men are free everything is possible. The challenges that America faces can be overcome by a free America, a democratic America. When I became President of Costa Rica, I began an alliance for liberty and democracy in the Americas. I said then, and I repeat now, that neither in politics or economics should we be aligned with governments that oppose their people. Latin America has never known a single war between two democracies. This reason alone is sufficient for all men of good faith, and all nations of good faith, to aid the effort to end tyrannies.

There Is an Urgency in America

There is an urgency for America to be free. All America must be free. I come from a world of great problems, which we are going to overcome in liberty. I come from a world with a feeling of urgency, because hunger has urgency. Violence that has overcome hope has urgency. Ideology which has betrayed dialogue has urgency. I come from a world where we have to be urgent in order to make it impossible to turn back from the path of liberty, and to frustrate all kinds of oppression. I come from a world which has urgency for the guerrilla and soldier to cease fighting: the young are dying, brothers are dying, and to-morrow they will not know why. I come from a world which has an urgency for the doors of the jails to open, so that the men held within will be able to leave, like yesterday, and be free.

America has an urgency for liberty, an urgency for democracy, and needs the understanding of the entire world to free itself of the dictator, and to free itself of misery.

I Am a Central American

I receive this prize as one of 27 million Central Americans. More than 100 years of pitiless dictators, injustice, and widespread poverty, precede the democratic awakening in Central America. Either to live in violence for another century, or reach a peace overcoming the fear of liberty; this is the challenge facing my little America. Only peace can write a new history.

In Central America, we are not going to lose faith. We are going to change history. How sad it is that they wish to have us believe that peace is a dream, that justice is a utopia, that it is not possible to share well being! How sad that there are those in the world who do not understand that in Central America, where there were plantations, today nations affirm the principle that they are looking for a better destiny for their people! How sad that there are those who do not understand that Central America does not want to prolong its past, but rather to write a new future, with hope for the young and dignity for the elderly.

To Convert Dreams into Realities

The isthmus of Central America is an area of great contrasts, but also of many similarities. Millions of men and women share dreams of liberty and development. These dreams evaporate in some countries in the face of systematic violations of human rights; they are smashed against fratricidal wars in the countryside and the cities, and they are affronted by the realities of severe poverty which paralyze the heart. Poets, who are the pride of humanity, know that millions upon millions cannot read their works in their own lands, because there are thousands upon thousands of men and women who are illiterate. There are in this narrow stretch of land painters and sculptors whom we have always admired, but also dictators we hate to remember, because they have offended the dearest values of man.

Central America does not want to, nor can it continue to, dream. History demands that those dreams become realities. There is no time to lose. Today we can take destiny in our own hands. In these lands, which cover at the same time the oldest and strongest democracy of Latin America—Costa Rica—and the history of the most pitiless and cruel dictators, the democratic awakening demands a special faithfulness to liberty.

As those dictators of yesterday were only capable of creating misery and mutilating hope, how absurd it is to pretend to cure those ills with a dictatorship of one extreme or another! In Central America no one has the right to fear liberty, no one has the right to preach absolute truths. The ills of one ideology are also the ills of the other ideology. All of them are enemies of the creativity of man. As Pascal said: "We know a great deal when we are skeptics. We know very little when we are ideologists."

History can only have a direction toward liberty. History can only have a soul of justice. When history moves against its natural path, it follows the route of shame, poverty, and oppression. There is no revolution if there is no liberty. All oppression moves in a direction opposed to the soul of man.

Liberty: Shared Eagerness

Central America finds itself at a terrible crossroads: Facing anguishing problems of poverty, there are some from the hilltops, or from governments, who look for dictatorships of other types, ignoring the clamor of liberty over the course of many generations. Then, in the context of these serious problems of widespread misery, problems defined in a North-South context, surfaces the conflict of East versus West. Where the problems of poverty are joined with an ideological struggle, the fear of liberty, Central America embodies a cross which bears dire predictions.

Let us not be mistaken. Only freedom from misery and fear is the answer for Central America, the answer for poverty, the answer for its political challenges. Those who, in the name of certain ideologies, advocate the solution to centuries of problems, only make the problems of yesterday even greater in the future.

There is a shared eagerness in the souls of men that asks from centuries past for liberty in Central America. No one should betray the alliance of these souls. To do so would condemn our small America to another 100 years of horrendous oppression, to another 100 years of death without meaning, another 100 years of struggle for liberty.

I Am a Costa Rican

I receive this prize as one of 2.7 million Costa Ricans. My country breathes its sacred liberty between two oceans which are its borders to the east and west. To the south and north, Costa Rica has almost always been bounded by dictatorships. We are a people without weapons, and we struggle to remain a people without hunger.

"ONLY PEACE CAN WRITE A NEW HISTORY"

We are for America a symbol of peace, and we wish to be a symbol of development. We hope to demonstrate that peace is a requirement, and a fruit, of development.

Land of Teachers

My land is a land of teachers. For that reason, it is a land of peace. We discuss our successes and failures with complete openness. Because mine is a land of teachers, we closed the army barracks and our children march with books under their arms, not with rifles on their shoulders. We believe in dialogue, in negotiation, in looking for a consensus. We repudiate violence. Because mine is a land of teachers, we believe in convincing, not vanquishing, our adversary. We prefer to raise the fallen, not oppress him, because we believe that no one has absolute truth. Because mine is a land of teachers, we look for an economy in which men cooperate together, and not an economy in which men compete to annihilation.

For the past 118 years in my land, education has been obligatory and free. Today medical care protects all citizens, and public housing is a fundamental tenet of my government.

A New Economy

In the same way that we are proud of our many successes, we do not hide our anguish, and our problems. In difficult times, we must be capable of establishing a new economy, to continue growth. We have said that we do not want an economy which is insensitive to domestic demands, or the demands of the most humble. We have said that in the name of economic growth, we are not going to renounce our dreams for a more egalitarian society. Today we are the nation with the lowest rate of unemployment in the Western hemisphere. We hope to be the first nation in Latin America which eliminates slums. We are convinced that a country free of slums will be a country free of hatred, that working for progress and liberty can also be a privilege of poor countries.

In these bitter years for Central America, many in my nation feared that Central American violence could contaminate Costa Rica, pushed by sick minds and blind fanaticism. Some Costa Ricans were so overcome by the fear that we would have to create an army, to keep the violence away from our doors. Such mindless weakness! These thoughts are worth less than the 30 pieces of silver handed over to Judas. The fortress of Costa Rica, the force which makes it invincible against violence, and that makes it more powerful than a thousand armies, is the force of liberty, of its roots, of the great ideals of our civilization. When these ideas are lived honestly, when one is not afraid of liberty, one is invulnerable against all totalitarians.

In Costa Rica we know that only liberty allows us to build political structures within which all people of the country can participate. Only liberty permits the tolerance to reconcile men. The painful paths of exile traveled throughout the world by Cubans, Nicaraguans, Paraguayans, Chileans, and so many others, not able to return to their own countries, are the cruelest testimony of an empire of ideology. Liberty does not have last names, and democracy has no colors. One realizes them where one finds them, within the real life of a people.

A Plan of Peace

Facing the violence in Central America, Costa Rica and all its history, Costa Rica and especially the idealism of a young nation, all demanded that I take to the field of battle in the region the peace of my people, the faith in dialogue, and the necessity for tolerance. As a servant of my people, I proposed a plan for Central America. This plan also was the basis of Simon Bolívar's cry for freedom, expressed in the valiant work of the Contadora Group and the Group of Aid.

I Am One of Five Presidents

I receive this prize as one of five presidents who have committed before the world the will of their people to change a history of oppression for a future of liberty; to change a history of hunger for a destiny of progress; to change the weeping of mothers and the violent death of their young into hope for a path of peace that we can travel together.

Hope is the strongest force which moves people. A hope that transforms, that makes new realities, is that which opens the way for the liberty of man. To encourage hope, it is necessary to unite courage and knowledge. Only then is it possible to avoid violence, only then is it possible to have the serenity needed to respond to aggression with peace.

There are occasions when, no matter how important and noble the crusade is, many eagerly attempt to undermine it. Some few seem to accept war as a normal course of things, as a solution to all problems. How ironic that the strongest forces are upset when the movement toward war is interrupted, when one works to destroy the reasons that feed hatreds! How ironic that trying to stop war is a policy which angers and attacks these people, as if we were trying to disturb a just dream, a necessary policy, and not a strangling ill! How ironic that the forces of peace enable many to discover that hatred is stronger than love, that the desire to reach power through military victories leads to a loss of reason for so many men, makes them have no shame, and makes them betray history.

All Fighting Should Stop

In Central America, five presidents have signed an accord to search for a firm and lasting peace. We are looking to silence weapons, and let men speak. These are conventional weapons which are killing our children, these are conventional weapons which are killing our youth.

The threat of a nuclear war, those fears which are described as a nuclear holocaust, seem to have made us insensitive to conventional warfare. The memory of Hiroshima is stronger than the memory of Vietnam! With how much desire do we want there to exist in the world the same respect for using conventional weapons as the atomic bomb? And in the same way, to kill many little by little, day by day, should be as reprehensible as killing many in one day. Do we live in a world so irrational that if all nations had the power of the atomic bomb, and the destiny of the world depended on one madman, that we would have more respect for conventional weapons? Would universal peace be more sure? Do we have a right to forget the 78 million human beings who have fallen in the wars of the 20th century?

Today the world is divided between those who live in fear of nuclear destruction, and those who fear, day-in and day-out, death by conventional weapons. The terror of the Holocaust is so big, that it has created a fearsome insensitivity about using subatomic arms. It is urgent—a demand of the intellect and a mandate of pity—that we struggle equally so that there will be neither a Hiroshima, nor a Vietnam.

"ONLY PEACE CAN WRITE A NEW HISTORY"

Weapons are not fired by themselves. Those who have lost hope are those who fire. Those are the ones who are dominated by the zealots. Those are the ones who fire the weapons. We must unceasingly fight for peace, and accept without fear those challenges of a world without hope and under the threat of the fanatic.

I Tell the Poet

The peace plan that we the five presidents signed faces all these challenges. The path of peace is difficult, very difficult. In Central America we need the help of all to reach peace.

It is easier to predict defeat than victory for peace in Central America. It is always easier to predict defeat than victory. That's how it was when man wished to fly, and also when he wished to conquer space. That's the way it was during the hard days of the two world wars of this century. And that's the way it is when man faces the most terrible diseases, during the work to end poverty and hunger in the world.

History has not been written by men who predicted failure, who denied a dream, who abandoned their beliefs, who permitted laziness to put intelligence to sleep. And if there were at certain times men who in solitude were looking for victories, there was always, vigilant, at their sides, the soul of their countries, the faith and destiny of generations.

Perhaps it was during difficult times for Central America, like the times in which we live, perhaps it was in anticipating today's crossroads, that Rubén Dario, the greatest poet of our America, wrote these words, convinced that history would change its course:

Pray generously, piously, proudly,
pray chastely, purely, celestially, courageously;
intercede for us, beg for us
because we are nearly without sap, without
buds
without soul, without life, without light,
    without Quixote,
    without feet, without wings, without Sancho
        and without God.

I assure the immortal poet that we are not going to stop dreaming, that we are not going to fear knowledge, that we are not going to flee from liberty. I tell the poet that always in Central America, we are not going to forget Quixote, we are not going to renounce life, we are not going to turn our backs on the soul, and we are never going to lose faith in God.

I am one of five men who signed an accord, a commitment that consists, in large part, in the act of desiring peace with all one's soul.

CHAPTER TEN

One More Spin

Rubén Dario, Quixote, the soul of peace, the momentum of history, Vietnam in the context of Hiroshima, a democratic awakening to replace dictators who shame humanity, the ongoing struggle against inequality and oppression—all portrayed in lyrical terms, all captured in Central America and carried to Norway of all places to be presented before a select committee whose only power is its moral authority . . .

Stop. This is not the stuff of government. This is the stuff of philosophers and poets, novelists and dreamers. This is abstraction and fiction, not the exercise of power as we know and understand it. This is child's play, an international stroll through the flowers, a pretty picture that ignores the dirty hard work of real gristle and muscle that powers foreign diplomacy as the big boys play it, with real armies, weapons, threats, and economic reprisals. This is the stuff of luxurious, protected fantasy.

But this is the stuff of Costa Rica. Without being overly romantic or indulgent of the faults of the place, one can celebrate the way the culture, and the president, have held onto hopes and dreams that rise above brutal cynicism. It is heartening to hear the way this sober national leader can use such grandiose imagery without having the words lodge in his throat because the hypocrisy is too large to swallow, to see a vision that marries democracy and justice with materialism and free enterprise to offer a Latin alternative, to appreciate how the intellectual statesman in a business suit can stand toe to toe with the fiery revolutionary in olive fatigues and trade punches about anything—from savvy superpower strategy to the living standards of his people to the righteous motivation of his policy—without having to back up.

There is a qualifying sense that Costa Rica can accomplish small wonders only because its big neighbor to the north has been relatively benign and protective. We send them money to bolster their economy, masking the fact that the much-celebrated Costa Rican standard of living is not truly supported by the Costa Rican economy. We afford them the luxury of an armyless state because the word is out that to mess with them is to mess with us.

Does that make Costa Rica's achievements less valid, the message of its president less profound? I don't think so. What it really means is that we have a success on our hands despite all the wobbling and veering of our policies. What it means is that we have a Central American ally we can support without having to look the other way, without

having to offer rationalizations about the strategic importance of the location, without having to conjure up false
certificates of human rights progress, without having to
share the unpopular brunt of popular uprisings, without
worrying about what form of suppression and control is
reasonable enough to appear on the evening news and not
provoke cries of outrage.

So rather than taking this little oasis for granted, ex-
pecting a cowered subservience, threatening economic
blackmail over policy disagreements, I think we should
advertise and applaud Costa Rica as an outpost of the
West. They have satisfied all our stated preconditions for
wholehearted support on the strength of their exemplary
democracy. It would represent a maturity in our world
view to engage in such a positive celebration and reinforcement—not to mention serving our true interests better: If the old domino theory has any credibility, then use
the example of Costa Rica's egalitarian tilt, well subsidized
and well publicized, to encourage other countries in the
same direction.

In this context, the embarrassed, half-hearted congratulations offered Oscar Arias by the United States government upon his winning the Nobel Peace Prize seem
ironic. By all rights this should have been an award we
not only applauded, but virtually shared. By all rights the
prize should have symbolized that the military might and
foreign diplomacy of the United States can indeed accomplish what our politicians claim is our highest mission:
protecting freedom and democracy wherever they can be
found. Where else in the developing world have democracy and capitalism better managed to coexist without the
scourge of abject poverty? What other Latin leader, in
terms of the rules of his election and his vision of states-

manship, more comfortably suits our best image of ourselves, our allies, and our influence? The Reagan administration perceived the Nobel award as a backhanded slap at its policies, but in the much bigger scheme of things it was a deep affirmation of United States ideals.

These are the implications of Costa Rica, this is the message in a bottle that is finally washing to our shore. This is what makes even the mundane experiences of that country, the common courtesies, the take-it-for-granted daily life, merge into the profound. As a close brush with death heightens the joys of simple living, the basic fabric of Costa Rican life weaves into a tapestry made more wonderful by the close brush of despair around it. To go anywhere at any time, to talk with anyone about anything, to eat here or there and know that you do not eat alone, to have a job and be paid to do it, to be sure your family will be in your home, under your roof, at the end of the day, these are the aspects of life that become all-important the instant they are threatened. Such threats pervade Central America, but they do not dominate Costa Rica. In most countries the platitudes of the leaders far outstrip the experiences of most people, but in Costa Rica the best sense of the place is the simplest, broadest, everyday stamp of life. It gives integrity to the slogans, and puts meat on the bones of the ideology.

And so, before I left, I wanted to take one more spin around the national block. It would be something of a litmus test, a reality check, a complete physical.

Traffic was stop-and-go on the way out of San José— and then there was a roadblock. Well, actually two teenagers were holding a piece of rope across the street, using the makeshift technique to induce people to give spare change to benefit handicapped children. They were part of a twenty-four-hour telethon, in a country where nearly 90 percent of the homes have televisions. I paid their good-hearted blackmail, preferring Costa Rica's version of a roadblock to all the others I have seen.

Downtown in Heredia, a block from a handsome church, the manager of a local *soda* regaled me with stories about the town. Her name was Marlen Arias Gutiérrez. I had stopped asking all the Ariases I bumped into whether they were related to the president, but this time I didn't have to ask, Marlen quickly assured me that she is. I was skeptical. Next thing I knew she had her official documents out: "It's a distant relation, and we're the poor side of the family," she allowed, but here's how it supposedly works: Oscar's father, Juan Rafael, was the brother of the father of Jesús Maria Arias Arias, who is Marlen's father. Got it? And would you like to see the family finca, just a few minutes outside of town?

I drove out of Heredia, into the Costa Rican equivalent of suburbia, and turned down a dirt driveway. There was the small home of Marlen's family, and stretching out behind it was acre after acre of bright green coffee plants shaded by the broad leaves of bananas. The men of Marlen's extended family greeted me and talked about coffee, how the Brazilian plant is tougher than the Colombian but doesn't produce as tasty a bean. The women of the family asked about religious life in the United States between sips of a special wine opened for an unexpected guest. I tried to explain my belief in a spirit, not necessarily a God, which seems to unite everything, a force I sensed at work, not necessarily a consciousness that has any awareness of human beings. I couldn't know if the concept was too atheistic and abstract, or my Spanish was too bad, but the idea didn't seem to get across.

ONE MORE SPIN

What did come across was a reminder of how intimate this country remains, both to its land and its leaders. From the street it's easy to miss how so many Costa Ricans remain rooted, how their backyards are so often small farms. And it's easy to forget how short the distance is, in every way, from a small finca like this to the Presidential House.

A few hours later I was racing up the Pan-American Highway. Within a month or two the fires that annually rage across the Guanacaste flatlands, set by ranchers to clear pasture land, would turn the tall green savanna grass into black stubble. But now the plains were peacefully waving and swooshing in the breeze. There were butterflies everywhere, particularly small white ones that danced across the road. Mile after mile, the car seemed to smash thousands of them, but there always were more. It was such a shame to kill so many of them, and so ironic, because the person I was driving to see had made his way here more than twenty-five years ago in large part because he had an abiding love affair with butterflies.

When I found Dan Janzen he was sitting on the porch of the small cabin in the national park at Santa Rosa where he lives much of the year. It is a ramshackle hut on a dirt road, a long way from the University of Pennsylvania, where he is a tenured professor. Plastic bags lined the frame of the porch like Christmas decorations, only each one held some species of larva or caterpillar whose secrets would be revealed when wings sprouted in solitary confinement. Inside, the house was strewn with scientific materials, books, clothing, and the researcher's best friend, a computer. Dan was sitting among all of this, shirtless, talking to a young park ranger he was training. You'd never know he was the winner of the Crafoord Prize, the

Swedish equivalent of the Nobel, recognizing him as one of the world's premier scientists. You'd never know that he has committed the rest of his life to saving what is known as the dry tropical forests around Santa Rosa. And you'd never know that by throwing down the gauntlet, negotiating with everyone from Guanacaste ranchers to New York City corporate executives, he is creating Guanacaste National Park, one of the last refuges for this kind of environment in the world, at four hundred square miles the largest park of its kind in the hemisphere.

Janzen knew early on that his best hope for convincing local landowners to support such a radical conservation strategy lay in the best aspects of the society. "It's a unique fact of Costa Rican culture," he said. "Here, if you catch somebody doing something wrong on your land, he stands there and argues with you, he tries to convince you it's okay what he's doing. In Nicaragua, El Salvador, and other places I've worked, he will either pick up a machete and attack you, or drop everything and run like hell. And this key difference made me feel we could get really far with a rational conservation argument."

Rationality has taken Janzen far. A key dozen or more Costa Rican families in the area have agreed to sell their land. Meanwhile, Janzen has worked out an innovative funding scheme: Costa Rica has a huge national debt, which the lending banks worry will never be repaid, so the banks are willing to discount that debt in return for cash in hand (something is better than nothing is the thought). If you have $270,000 to offer, the banks will write off a full $1 million of Costa Rican debt. The Costa Rican government obviously would love to see this happen, so much so that it is willing to issue government bonds for roughly $750,000 to anyone who will give

$270,000 to wipe out the $1 million debt. So Janzen raised $270,000 from wildlife supporters, used that money to buy off $1 million of Costa Rican national debt, received $750,000 in government bonds, and used the bonds to buy the land in Guanacaste. Costa Rica has its debt reduced, Janzen gets triple his buying power, and land is put into conservation—all in one rational fell swoop.

Janzen's fight is not over. Money is hard to come by, and the burning and cutting of Guanacaste continues. But he knows the effort is worth it and he knows that his choice to make a stand in Costa Rica, of all places, was right. Like the Quakers at Monteverde, he has influenced the course of Costa Rica in this generation. Yet like a moth to a flame, he was overwhelmingly attracted to the country by its society as much as the natural beauty he is trying to protect.

"All the money pouring into Costa Rica for conservation over the last twenty years has not come because of the biological richness," he says. "Oh sure, that richness has to be there, but it is also there in many other places. The difference is that people have faith that the money will be used well. It won't go down a rat hole. That's the real reason. The naturalists and the government here say, 'Send us funding to save X thousand species.' They don't say, 'Do it because the Costa Rican government will protect your investment.' But everyone knows it will."

The adjectives biologists around the world are using to describe Janzen's work—heroic, unique, historic, visionary—sound a lot like the adjectives people use to describe Costa Rica as a whole. And, as Janzen implies, that's no mere coincidence.

Out of the park, a few miles down the coast, *Playa del Coco* (Coco Beach) was a small honky-tonk of a getaway that Dan Janzen would not think represents the best in environmental land use. But then again, the bars and discos and small homes that line the crescent of dark sand certainly make many people happy. Makeshift soccer games were in progress, the goals nothing more than two sticks in the sand. Costa Ricans like to burrow into the sand, letting it cake up all over them until they have a good excuse to get into the water and wash it off. A rickety old pier was a strolling diversion, a few fishing boats were moored and sheltered within the cup of the half-moon of the beach, and prehistoric-looking pelicans patrolled above deeper water, waiting for the silver flash of a fish to urge them into a bombing dive. I could count on that being the only aggressive display I would see all afternoon. It was Sunday, families and friends lay in the sand. This, I thought, is sound public policy.

A day later, far down the coast near Quepos, I found public policy priorities expressed in the crown jewel of national parks on the Pacific Coast, Manuel Antonio. Costa Ricans played volleyball and soccer in front of a few small restaurants, while other stretches of beach provided no more amenities than almond trees for shade and white sand for turquoise surf. This was not some retreat for rich foreigners only, this is where Costa Ricans go to get away from it all. The beauty of the place, like the beauty of Costa Rica, is compounded by its being both egalitarian and accessible.

South of Limón, barely twenty miles from the border with Panama, the national park at Cahuita is the Atlantic's symmetrical counterpart to Manuel Antonio. Hippies from around the world still find their way to the little town at the edge of the park, spending their days on the tropical beach that wraps seven miles around Cahuita

Point, spending their nights in small bars buying mari-
juana from local hustlers, listening to reggae, and watching old men play dominoes. It was a replay of a scene from
the sixties. Two Italian women with French boyfriends
were working their way toward Brazil, selling handmade
jewelry as they went, to finance the trip.

Even Cahuita is booming now, with a new road, new
construction, and the pristine park as a tourist draw. What
was a dirty, ragged, neglected town has now been tied
into the Costa Rican economy. Much is gained, much is
lost; the scenario has been played out thousands of times,
from Cape Cod to Key West to Cancún. Now it is
Cahuita's turn to evolve into a profit center.

Few if any roads have yet found their way north of
Limón along this coast, where boats replace cars. An inland
waterway system and canal stretches sixty miles to the Nicaraguan border. A national park is up there, named after
the green turtle that lays its eggs along the shore. Even *la
tortuga verde* finds refuge in Costa Rica, like so many ex-
iles and refugees of every stripe; scientists say that this may
be the last shoreline on the western side of the Caribbean
where the turtles can lay their eggs in peace. The government is trying to figure out how to deal with more and
more tourists who are making their way up the waterways
to look at the turtles, threatening the very creatures they
have come to see. In the scheme of things, it is only one of
the many balancing acts Costa Rica must manage.

Speaking of recent arrivals, I managed to return to San
José in time to make it to the weekly "Newcomers' Semi-
nar," held at the Hotel Irazu. Fifteen people were in the
hall, all North Americans, mostly of retirement age. "I
love the way the men kiss the older women on the cheek

like that," one newcomer said to another as they took their seats. "It's so warm and friendly."

The Honorary President of the Pensionado and Rentista Association began the meeting by explaining the laws that encourage people to choose Costa Rica instead of Florida for their golden years. "Law 4812, established in 1972, promotes retirees to come to Costa Rica, not to get into the work force, but to give Costa Rica a dollar income straight into the economy," he stated. Shrewd, open-armed, the idea has all the markings of the president who signed it into law, José Figueres.

The newcomers heard all the ins and outs, the differences between being a *pensionado* and a *rentista* (a rentista can still work, but loses other benefits), the vagaries of exit visas and land registration rituals, the quality of health care (considered to be as good as that of many developed nations). But what really has been selling these people on Costa Rica are scenes like the one in progress at La Sabana, the largest park of San José, a few blocks away.

It was a holiday (as seems to be the case so often), this one to celebrate the Immaculate Conception, and many people were taking advantage of the time off for some open space and sunshine. Ever-present bicyclists zoomed by on their gleaming machines, Fellini-esque interruptions of the city pastoral. As always, a pick-up soccer game was in progress; a preteen goalie wore a T-shirt that read, "Ollie 6, Congress 0."

Seated on benches, rocking baby carriages, young men and women were discussing the latest scandal to mushroom: allegations that some public officials had taken United States AID money for personal use instead of national benefit. One charge was that young relatives of former President Monge were given some of the money to help pay their college tuitions. The charges were serious (though unproven); they had the makings of a scandal, but then again, a military dictator in next-door Panama stood accused of moving tens of millions of dollars in cocaine profits to his private Swiss bank account. In Costa Rica, the figure is tens of thousands of dollars, and the money might be going toward college educations.

A vendor rustled up some *gallo pinto*, rice and beans. The snack became a fine excuse to sit and watch the world go by: admire a baby asleep on a blanket, stare at some strangely modern abstract sculpture on a hill, follow the progress of bubbles blown off the classic little plastic stick with a round end, wonder how long a couple can kiss before coming up for air, marvel at the quick if short Latin basketball players, and allow the feeling of oasis that is La Sabana within San José, that is Costa Rica within Central America, to overtake everything else.

My thoughts drifted toward Arias, whose home was only a few blocks away. He had been celebrated and feted in Europe after the Nobel ceremonies, making a point of stopping in Denmark to see his European prototype of Costa Rican society. He returned home exhausted with a heavy cold from the harsh winter weather. Costa Rica did not afford him much of a respite: A scandal erupted about rich people escaping car import fees even as the middle class struggled with higher taxes, while Arias's personal popularity plummeted in direct proportion to rising taxes and to people's sense that their president had become perhaps a little too much of a big shot. Calderón and the anti-Liberacionistas already were being proclaimed the sure winners of the next election.

It was business as usual, rough-and-tumble democracy. It was time for the stubborn, pragmatic side of Arias to assert itself, to prove he could have his feet in the clay while his head was in the clouds, to juggle the egos of party politics with a role in negotiations to remove Noriega from power in Panama, to try to put as much care into a speech before Costa Rica's Congress as into the commencement address at Harvard University in June. The Nobel Prize had elevated Arias to a dizzy height, but with that came the danger that his domestic fall from grace could be that much farther. The man's work ethic needed to flex; he had to get his hands dirty in the politics of Costa Rica. And that remains the challenge of his final year in office.

Yet no one smirks anymore at his ambitions, grandiose as they seem, because two of the three have already been accomplished: becoming president of Costa Rica, winning the Nobel Peace Prize, and serving as secretary general of the United Nations. And no one doubts that Oscar Arias, like Figueres before him, will be a dominant force in Costa Rican politics for the rest of his life.

It certainly would have been easy to while away the rest of the day in the luxury of the park, appreciating Costa Rica's greatest domestic product—peaceful tranquility. But I had miles to go before I could sleep. At the corner of the park near the national museum, I flagged a cab. "Juan Santamaría," I said.

"Leaving Costa Rica?" asked the cabbie.

"Unfortunately, yes."

"My sister lives in New York," he said, talkative and aggressive as any cabbie anywhere, battling through a traffic light to get onto the *autopista*. "She likes it all right, but me, I'd never move. Leave Costa Rica, for what? I own this cab, I live in a nice place, and we have a style, you know what I mean? A quality of life, let's say. We celebrate our holidays, yes? In the United States, my

248

sister says people don't really know how to celebrate Christmas or Election Day. Here, we celebrate."

I allowed he had a point.

"People think the United States is so great, and it is great," he pushed on. "Don't get me wrong, I love the United States. But I love Costa Rica, too. I wouldn't want to move, not me, no sir. Keep the Nicaraguans up north, keep Panama's troubles down south, and I'll stay right where I am."

Sounded all right to me. And very Costa Rican. As we swung around the cloverleaf into the airport, I was thinking that nationalism is not always an evil. As I paid the cab fare, exchanging good lucks, I was realizing how important it is for a country to give its people pride in themselves, and how great it is when that pride does not have to evolve into militarism. As they called my flight I wondered whether Costa Rica would remain an anomaly, a weirdly pacific blip on the curve of Central American history, whether its values would translate across its borders or, on the contrary, whether it would even be able to stand up to the pressures all around it. As we taxied to the runway, I caught a final glimpse of the purple mountains that ring San José and thought about the levels of complexity and diversity of this little place, how easy it is to say two words—*Costa Rica*— conjure up an image—small Central American country— and then dismiss the variety and pageantry of a culture. And as we took off for Miami, for that big *Estados Unidos* up north, I wondered if North Americans were ready to look into the pocket mirror which Costa Rica holds up and to learn something from a tiny country that takes our own ideals seriously, and insists on waging peace.

NOTES

1. Mario Boza and Rolando Mendoza, *The National Parks of Costa Rica,* trans. Susana Heringman (Madrid: The Costa Rican Institute of Tourism, The National Park Service, The National Open University, and The National University, 1981), 30–33.

2. *The Tower Commission Report: The Full Text of the President's Special Review Board* (New York: Times Books and Bantam Books, 1987), 472.

3. Charles D. Ameringer, *Don Pepe: A Political Biography of José Figueres of Costa Rica* (Albuquerque: University of New Mexico Press, 1978), 19.

4. Kent Britt, "Costa Rica Steers the Middle Course," *National Geographic,* vol. 160, no. 1 (July 1981): 40.

NOTES

5. José Figueres Ferrer, *Cartas a un Ciudadano* (San José: Imprenta Nacional, 1956), 110.

6. Ameringer, *Don Pepe*, 146.

7. Alan Riding, "For Rudderless Costa Rica, a Quixotic Rescue Effort," *The New York Times* (January 12, 1981): A2.

8. Arthur Herzog, *Vesco*, (New York: Doubleday, 1987), 245.

9. *The Tico Times*. Published weekly by Richard Dyer. San José. May 17, 1985.

10. Clark Spencer, "Costa Rica: Central Illinoisans Pioneer on War's Edge," *The State Journal Register*, covering Central Illinois (February 22, 1984), 7.

11. Jonathan Kwitney, "Rancher in Costa Rica Was Big Help to U.S. Against the Sandinistas," *The Wall Street Journal* (May 21, 1987): 1.

12. Spencer, "Costa Rica: Central Illinoisans Pioneer," 11.

13. *The Tico Times*, March 1, 1985.

14. Ibid, June 6, 1986.

15. Kwitney, "Rancher in Costa Rica Was Big Help to U.S.," 1.

16. Martha Honey and Tony Avirgan, *La Penca: Report of an Investigation* (Martha Honey and Tony Avirgan, 1985), 1–2.

17. Leslie Cockburn, *Out of Control* (New York: Atlantic Monthly Press, 1987), 172.

18. *The Tico Times*, October 18, 1985.

19. Ibid, July 31, 1987.

20. Ibid, May 24, 1985.

21. Ibid.

22. Ibid, February 7, 1986.

23. *The Tower Commission Report*, 470.

24. Ibid, 473.

25. Ibid.

26. Montgomery Brower and Garry Clifford, "Nobel Winner Oscar Arias Makes Costa Rica and Mouse that Roared for Peace in Latin America," *People* (November 9, 1987), 58.

NOTES

27. Harry Anderson, Timothy Noah, Robert Parry, and Charles Lane, "The Nobel Difference," *Newsweek* (October 26, 1987), 44.

28. "Presidente Fustigó Ayer a La Nación," *La Nación* (June 7, 1987): 4A.

29. Ibid, December 10, 1987. "En pos de un sueño," by Eugenia Sancho. p 1 of "Viva, revista diaria de La Nacion."

30. Edgar Espinoza, "Nuestros dos papás," *La Nación* (June 7, 1987): 14.

31. Ibid. "Rumbos paralelos," *La Nación* (December 11, 1987), 14A.

The following materials provided background, insight, and corroboration:

1. Anderson, Jon Lee. "A CIA Man in Nicaragua." *Life Magazine,* February 1985.

2. Bird, Leonard A. *Costa Rica, a Country Without an Army.* Leeds, England: Northern Friends Peace Boards, 1978.

3. Blake, Beatrice and Anne Becher. *The New Key to Costa Rica.* San José, 1986.

4. Booth, John A. "Costa Rican Democracy." In *Democracy in Developing Countries.* Ed. Larry Diamond, Juan Linz, and Seymour Martin Lipset. Boulder, CO: Lynne Rienner, 1988.

5. Costa Rican Chamber of Commerce. *Investors' Guide to Costa Rica.* San Jose: Costa Rican Chamber of Commerce, 1985.

6. Denton, Charles F. *Patterns of Costa Rican Politics.* Boston: Allyn and Bacon, 1971.

7. English, Burt. *Liberación Nacional in Costa Rica.* Gainesville: University of Florida Press, 1971.

8. Goldrich, Daniel. *Sons of the Establishment: Elite Youth in Panama and Costa Rica.* Chicago: Rand McNally, 1966.

9. Government of Costa Rico. *The World's Most Peaceful Country.* Tourist pamphlet. Government of Costa Rica, 1937.

10. Ricardo Fernández Guardia. *The History of the Discovery and Conquest of Costa Rica.* Trans. Harry Weston Van Dyke. New York: Thomas Y. Crowell Co., 1913.

NOTES

11. Ricardo Fernández Guardia. *Cuento Ticos; Short Stories of Costa Rica*, Trans. Gary Casement. Cleveland: Burrows Brothers Co., 1925.

12. Guerra Tomás, *José Figueres: Una Vida Por la Justicia Social*. Heredia: Centro de Estudios Democraticos de América Latina, 1987.

13. Institute for Central American Studies. *Mesoamerica—News and Analysis of Central America*. San José, monthly publication.

14. Institute for the Comparative Study of Political Systems. *Costa Rica Election Factbook*. Washington D.C.: Institute for the Comparative Study of Political Systems, 1966.

15. National Security Council notes during the presidency of John F. Kennedy, entitled "Costa Rica." Dorchester: John F. Kennedy Presidential Library.

16. Regional Office of the High Commission on Refugees of the United Nations. *Situacion del Programa Para Refugiados en Costa Rica*. Regional Office of the High Commission on Refugees of the United Nations. 1986.

17. Sánchez, Oscar Arias. *Grupos de Presion en Costa Rica*. San José: Editorial Costa Rica, 1971.

18. Secretary of Information and Communication, Government of Costa Rica. *Disarmed Democracy*. Trans. by Carlos Silva. San Jose: Secretary of Information and Communication, 1983.

19. Young, Allen M. *Costa Rica: Nature, Prosperity and Peace on the Rich Coast*. Milwaukee: Interamerican Research Corporation, 1984.